How to
Understand and Manage
Public
Relations

GW00702177

How to
Understand and Manage

Public
Relations

A JARGON-FREE GUIDE TO
PUBLIC RELATIONS MANAGEMENT

DR. JON WHITE

CENTURY
BUSINESS

Copyright © Jon White 1991

The right of Jon White to be identified as the author of this
work has been asserted by him in accordance with the
Copyright, Designs and Patents Act 1988

First published in 1991 by
Business Books Limited
An imprint of Random Century Limited
20 Vauxhall Bridge Road, London SW1V 2SA

Random Century Australia (Pty) Limited
20 Alfred Street, Milsons Point, Sydney
New South Wales 2061, Australia

Random Century New Zealand Limited
9–11 Rothwell Avenue, Albany, Glenfield
Auckland 10, New Zealand

Century Hutchinson South Africa (Pty) Limited
PO Box 337, Bergvlei, South Africa

Typeset by Tek Art Ltd, Addiscombe, Croydon, Surrey
Printed and bound in Great Britain by
Mackays of Chatham PLC, Chatham, Kent

British Library Cataloguing in Publication Data
A catalogue record for this book is available from
the British Library

ISBN 0-09-174767-8 (Hbk)
ISBN 0-09-174766-X (Pbk)

To Carol-Ann

ACKNOWLEDGEMENTS

I should like to thank a number of individuals for their help in the preparation of this book, in particular David Walton. until recently with British Petroleum, for permission to use material which appears in Chapter 1 of the book; Gwes Lloyd, Corporate Identity Manager with the Prudential Corporation plc, for his help with the Prudential case referred to in the book; and Lucy Shankleman and Martin Liu at Business Books Limited for their encouragement.

I should also like to acknowledge the indirect contribution made by the many public relations practitioners who, over the years, have given their time to me, and to students with whom I have worked.

Dr Jon White
Cranfield School of Management

10 January, 1991

CONTENTS

INTRODUCTION

Public relations is now an important part of modern management, but for a number of reasons its full contribution to management is not realized.

This book sets out to help managers derive greater benefit from well-managed public relations activities. Its underlying argument is simply that public relations is as much a part of management as human resource management or financial management. Public relations is, quite literally, about the relationship between an organization and various 'publics' – employees, shareholders, customers and other groups. These relationships are one of an organization's most important resources; the work of the public relations practitioner is, therefore, vitally important.

We can probably all think of organizations which manage their public relations well. They are the organizations we trust and are familiar with, with which we feel comfortable and would want to do business. For the manager, the interesting question is: how do these organizations win respect and convince people that they are organizations to support? Performance is part of the answer: people will go back to organizations which have proven themselves and their products and services reliable. But there is more to it than performance. The most worthy company may find itself without support at time of crisis, because it has failed to build and sustain important relationships for occasions when they are needed.

This book explores the ways in which public relations is used to establish and maintain relationships. It emphasizes that relationships do not necessarily develop along satisfactory lines: their development has to be managed to support the interests, objectives, aspirations, products and services of the organization.

The approach to public relations taken in this book is intended to be practical and to provide managers with guidance towards making decisions regarding effective management of public relations activities. The book will look at the realistic placement of public relations in the overall management task and will help to answer questions about the allocation of resources to public relations activities: should staff be appointed within the organization to manage public relations activities, and what should be expected from them? If outside advisers are used, what sort of services should they provide and what sort of skills should they offer? How can the value of public relations advice and programmes be assessed?

These questions and others will be considered along with a review of some of the main areas of public relations practice. At the same time, the book will try to clear up some of the terms which are used to describe public relations practice. Confusion in the use of terms can obstruct discussion and management of public relations activities.

As far as possible, the book will provide decision checklists, summarizing points to be taken into consideration when public relations activities are to be incorporated into overall management plans.

I hope to communicate some of the excitement and interest involved in public relations practice. Public relations practitioners are fortunate in having to take a broad view of the interests of the organisations which they serve. They are obligated by their role to see organizations in a social context and if they are carrying out their role properly they are able to assess social issues and group interests in a way which enables them to 'import novelty' into the organizations they advise. It's this scope for contribution to organizational change, to management decision-making and to mutually beneficial social relationships which gives the practice its personal satisfactions for practitioners. For managers, the qualified, energetic public relations adviser can be among the most valued of counsellors. The public relations perspective itself is also of enormous value in management, since it complements and tempers other perspectives – such as those provided by specialists in financial management or marketing – brought to bear on management decisions and actions.

Public relations is not just the province of the business corporation. In the early 1990s, the value of the practice is being seen by many other organizations, such as educational institutions, charities, government departments and health care organizations. Nor is public relations only of concern to the large organization: small businesses and small community organizations also have to give thought to, and manage their important relationships. Their difficulties in the management of public relations have to do with lack of time and resources to devote to public relations activities.

This book is intended to help managers make better use of public relations, basing their public relations programmes and activities on an understanding of its real value in management.

Dr Jon White

CHAPTER ONE

PUBLIC RELATIONS' ROLE IN MANAGEMENT

'Meanwhile, few experts are able to define what PR is.'
The Times, 18 July 1990.[1]

'Corporate communications – as PR now calls itself – is more than mere window dressing or lunching hacks... the craft... is still in its infancy... companies know it is important but are not sure how to go about it or what skills it entails.'
The Economist, 16–24 March 1989.[2]

THERE IS, EVEN among public relations practitioners themselves, considerable confusion about what public relations is and what it has to offer. Some of this confusion can be traced back to a reluctance to use the term 'public relations' and to look directly at what public relations as a practice involves.

As a term to describe a number of management activities, public relations has become devalued in common use. The practice has lacked credibility from the outset because of its origins, in press agentry in the United States and in government propaganda and information work elsewhere. Press agentry aims for publicity and media mentions as ends in themselves, and may lead practitioners into practices which at best irritate media personnel and at worst verge on dishonesty. Media commentary on the 'public relations exercises' mounted by politicians and business organizations reinforce poor opinions of the practice. The image of public relations has not been

1

helped by the poor quality of service provided by the numbers of inadequately trained staff who have come into public relations in recent years as a result of the growth of the practice.

Now, reluctance to use the words 'public relations' leads organizations to employ other terms to describe the practice. This has the effect of adding to confusion, as other terms such as 'corporate communications' or 'public affairs' are used to describe public relations activities. As we will see later, these terms carry precise meaning and should be kept for the activities to which they refer.

Public relations practitioners sometimes idealize what they do, with definitions of the practice which stress quasi-educational goals. The British Institute of Public Relations, for example, defines public relations as:

'The planned and sustained effort to establish and maintain goodwill and mutual understanding between an organization and its publics'.

Other groups of practitioners claim that public relations is practised in the public interest. The Canadian Public Relations Society defines public relations as the management function which evaluates public attitudes, identifies the policies and procedures of an individual or organization with the public interest, and plans and executes a programme of action to earn public understanding and acceptance.

Despite the confusion over terms and reluctance to refer directly to public relations, the importance of the practice is recognized by managers. Sir John Harvey-Jones, a former chairman of the major British corporation ICI, suggested in the article from *The Economist* quoted at the head of this chapter that the main activities with which a company chairman should concern himself are strategic planning and public relations. Studies in the United States in the 1980s showed that senior managers are spending more of their time on activities which are clearly identifiable as public relations activities. Other studies, for example by the British polling organization, Market and Opinion Research International (MORI),[3] have indicated that, although managers are spending more time on public relations activities, their satisfaction with the advice and service they are getting from their public relations adivsers is low. The study by MORI carried out in 1987 for the Institute of Public Relations found that a substantial minority, 21 per cent, of industry leaders hold unfavourable views of public relations and regarded the practise less favourably than advertising or market research.

To cut through some of the confusion in terms which refer to public relations, the Public Relations Society of America established a special committee to review terms in current use. In a report[4] presented in October 1988 the committee concluded that there is no satisfactory alternative term to public relations. Although it carries the negative connotations that have been mentioned, the term is current and should be clearly understood. The report suggests that public relations is an overall term, which covers specialist areas of practice such as public affairs and corporate communications, and carries a broad meaning. The report offers several versions of this:

'Public relations helps an organization and its publics to adapt mutually to each other.'

'Public relations is an organization's efforts to win the co-operation of groups of people'.

'Public relations helps organizations effectively interact and communicate with their key publics'.

These definitions do get closer to a more realistic statement of what public relations has to contribute to management, by focussing on goals such as adaptation, co-operation and effective interaction. The achievement of these goals can be seen in behaviour – of members of groups of interest to an organization, of members of the organization itself, or both groups. This is an important consideration when we come to look at how public relations can be evaluated.

Public relations as a part of management

The aim of public relations practice is to have an effect on behaviour – on the behaviour of groups of people bound into relationships. As a practice, public relations makes use of communication to affect behaviour. Goodwill and understanding may be important points en route to influencing and changing behaviour, but they are not the end goals of public relations practice. To many people, this view of public relations suggests manipulation, which uses communication to persuade people to behave in ways that they would not otherwise. Some idealized views of public relations which claim noble purposes for the practice attempt to avoid accepting that the main aim of public relations is to influence behaviour.

Let's put this view of public relations into a management setting and then go on to look at a specific example of how this view applies in practice. Public relations' main aim is to influence behaviour, specifically the behaviour of groups in relation one to another. As a part of the overall management task, it is concerned with the management of important relationships – with government, the media, the community and groups who have special interests in the organization. These groups include employees. The behaviour of groups is influenced in order to support the achievement of organizational objectives.

The aims of public relations management are:

- To establish and sustain important relationships in order to influence the behaviour of groups of people involved
- To anticipate trends, issues or events which may be disruptive to those relationships and

- To take steps to minimize their impact

Properly managed public relations activities – attending to the interests of groups important to the organization, understanding their views, attitudes and opinions, and taking time to communicate with them – contribute to management in a number of important ways. They contribute to decision-making, by providing information to management about the views of groups inside and outside the organization. They also help the organization to be more responsive and senior managers to clarify objectives and directions for the organization, before communicating them to groups such as investors, customers or media commentators.

Public relations as a practical management discipline

Summary points
Public relations:

- Provides another perspective on the management task
- Involves the management of relationships (Aim: to have an influence on behaviour)
- Identifies, anticipates issues likely to have an impact on key relationships and responds to their development
- Contributes, within the organization, to planning, cohesion and effectiveness
- Involves managed communication

In this view of public relations, it's important to recognize that attempts to manage relationships and to influence behaviour affect the organization on whose behalf public relations is being practised, *as well as* groups outside the organization. If a public relations adviser sees a need for organizational change as a result of community feedback, then his or her obligation is to argue for such change (whether or not the arguments are accepted and acted upon remains a management prerogative).

Public relations management in British Petroleum

David Walton, until recently director of government and public affairs with British Petroleum (BP), a major British multinational oil company, used the graphic set out in Figure 1 to explain the role of public relations in management in the company, to the company's management groups. A similar graphic could be recreated for any organization, but Figure 1 identifies the groups important to BP.

The graphic shows that BP exists in the centre of a network of relationships. Some of the company's most important relationships are with groups found within the central area of the network: employees, shareholders, customers, suppliers and partners. The graphic also shows the importance of organizations which might be thought to be remote from the company's more immediate interests, such as international bodies like the United Nations.

The network also brings home the fact that groups important to the company are in relationship to each other. Pressure groups, such as environmental conservation groups, are able to communicate their point of view to – and to influence – government and the media, as well as public opinion.

David Walton's argument for a managed approach to public relations activities for the company stressed that BP pursues its interests and objectives in the social setting provided by these important relationships. The company's case has to be presented in this setting and it has to develop while taking account of the interests of other groups involved. If the company is not actively involved in the relationships shown, then they may develop in ways which would be unfavourable to the company's interests.

For some years, BP has been exploring for, and successful in locating, on-shore sources of oil in the UK. Pursuing the objective of developing on-shore resources, the company has had to contend with government, local community and pressure group interests. The task of public relations is to manage relationships, and the interests of groups involved in important relationships, so that objectives can be achieved. It is an enabling practice, which makes it easier for the organizations to identify and accommodate to interests at work in situations faced.

Public relations and other functions of management

The BP network of relationships (see Figure 1) also shows how public relations relates to other functions of management. Public relations is often thought of as part of marketing, but it is clear, looking at the BP network, that public relations is concerned with more than the relationship of the organization to its market place. Customers are immediately important to the organization, as it develops and places its products on the market. The relationship of BP to its customers is built within the context of other relationships, with the media, with government and with the general public.

Public relations is a complement – and a corrective – to marketing, providing support, but also a broader perspective which contributes to management decision-making and which may, on some occasions, argue against the narrower perspective of the marketing approach. We will come back to the relationship between public relations and marketing in Chapter 7.

Another important relationship for BP – and for any organization – is with its own employees. Employee relations are an established concern of personnel or human resource departments or specialists within organizations, but public relations can again complement their work.

Public relations' interest in employees is two-fold. First, employees' support is vital if an organization is to achieve its objectives. This support has to be won and re-won. Second, employees are representatives of the organization, and communicate on its behalf. They need to be aware of their roles as representatives of the organization, and knowledgeable about it, so that they can represent it adequately. Public relations' work with employees is directed towards informing them about the organization and its objectives, winning their support and

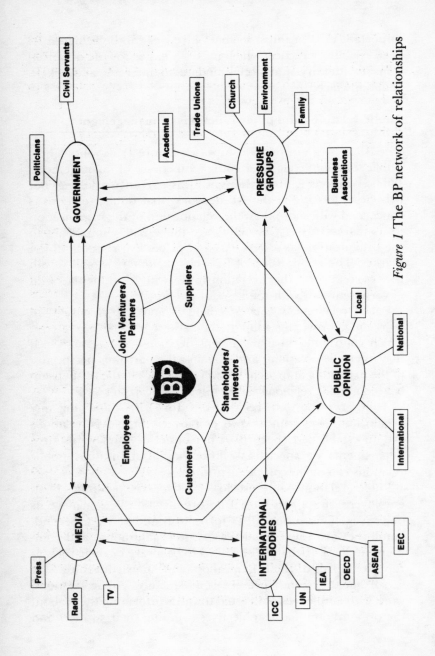

Figure 1 The BP network of relationships

encouraging them to act as effective representatives of the organization. This work has a different focus to it compared with the work carried out by personnel or human resource departments, but there is obvious scope for public relations to collaborate with these departments.

Public relations and other functions of management

Summary points

As a function of management, public relations will interact with other management functions:

- It may be supportive and complementary to personnel. Both have an interest in employee communications, but pursue different objectives in communicating with employees. Personnel's interest is in communicating details regarding conditions of employment, whereas public relations is concerned with winning employee support for organizational objectives and ensuring that they are sufficiently informed to be able to act as representatives of the organization

- It may also be supportive and complementary to marketing. Many of the communication techniques used in public relations are also used in marketing communications. In many organizations, the communication skills available in public relations departments, or from public relations staff may be drawn on directly by marketing to support product promotion. One of the tasks which may be allocated to public relations is that of creating a favourable environment for marketing activities. Other relationships – for example, with government, the media or with pressure groups – are managed so as to improve the likelihood that marketing activities will be successful

- Finance, planning, production and other departments should also be set against public relations to draw out possible areas of co-operation and conflict

Options for the management of public relations

If public relations is a task of management like others, what arrangements can be made for managing public relations activities? Managers who believe that it is an important part of the overall management task are faced with a number of options when it comes to providing resources for it. The 'lean and mean' approach favoured by many large corporations intent upon keeping central and support costs to a minimum may see the establishment of a one-person office as a suitable option, where the person appointed is able to draw on outside resources as required. The small business, or the charitable organization, may not have the resources to staff the function, and may rely on the time and interest of a senior manager to ensure that public relations activities are carried out.

Decisions on the most suitable approach to public relations will depend on:

- Knowledge of the options available, their advantages and disadvantages
- The requirement the organization has for public relations support
- The resources available to the organization – internal and external
- Management and staff attitudes towards public relations
- The experience the organization has had with public relations in the past
- The personality and interests of the organization's most senior manager

Options available – their advantages and disadvantages

There are five options for managing public relations activities:

- *The first option* – scarcely a true one given the consequences – is to do nothing about public relations. This approach has the advantage of incurring no immediate costs for the organization, but has the over-riding disadvantage that important relationships will develop in an unmanaged way, or – worse – will be developed by competitor organizations in ways more favourable to them

- *The second option* is to retain responsibility for public relations at the senior management level, to manage it through an allocation of senior management time and attention. The advantage of this approach is that public relations is a matter of direct senior management concern and the costs of staffing an internal department, or using outside resources are avoided. The disadvantages of this approach are that public relations may be overlooked as other demands on senior management time take precedence and that the senior manager given responsibility for public relations may not necessarily have the skills and knowledge to be effective in a public relations role

- *The third option* is the option chosen by most organizations. It involves making an internal staff appointment, or setting up an internal department to manage public relations activities. This option has a number of important advantages: the individual or staff group appointed can become thoroughly familiar with the organization, its environment, the issues of importance to it, and so on. As an internal resource, the department or individual appointed is readily available to the organization and can act quickly to support the organization's interests. A disadvantage of maintaining internal staff is the cost. Other disadvantages are that, over time, internal staff become too closely identified with the organization's perspective and objectives and that they lose their own perspective. Their own perspective is one of the main contributions public relations personnel have to offer the organizations for which they work

- *The fourth option* avoids some of the disadvantages of the previous option. It involves the use of external resources – public relations advisers and consultants, working from consultancies providing specialist public relations services.

The use of external resources avoids the costs of appointing and supporting internal staff. External staff have the advantage of an outside perspective and a broad exposure to a range of client problems. They are also capable of providing services otherwise unavailable to the organization. The main disadvantage of using external staff is that they need time to become familiar with the organization, its staff and requirements

■ *The fifth option* combines the advantages of internal and external options. It is chosen by larger organizations, but is an option open to any organization seeking to combine the advice and services of internal and external staff. External staff can add to the work of internal staff by providing an outside, objective view of the work of the internal group and the programmes and activities it manages. These can take on a life of their own and it is useful to have an outside group re-examine and assess long-established approaches and objectives. The disadvantage of this option is that it can be costly, although interventions by outside staff at the right time can save the organization money by reducing the costs of programmes and activities which have outlived their effectiveness

The five options are:

■ To do nothing and risk allowing competitors to determine the course of key relationships
■ To retain public relations as a senior management responsibility and allow for its management by a member of the senior management group
■ To delegate public relations to an internal staff member or staff department
■ To draw on the services of outside consultants
■ To use a combination of internal staff and outside consultants

The choice of option will depend on conclusions reached as

the organization's requirements for public relations support, its resources, attitudes and experience with public relations are considered.

Requirements for public relations support

All organizations have relationships to which they need to attend – with their own employees, and with outside groups, such as the members of the local communities in which they operate. Whether or not they need public relations support, through the allocation of senior management time and attention or the help of specialist internal or external staff, will depend on a number of factors. These include the turbulence of the social environment that the organization faces, the pressures bearing upon it, its own objectives and the opportunities and threats it can identify.

Turbulence is experienced in high levels of competition, government intervention in the economy and rapid social change brought on by international, political, economic and technological developments. Currently, turbulence is experienced by most organizations, even the smallest, as they cope with increased competition, economic uncertainty and social change such as change in the composition of the available workforce.

Pressure on organizations is also increasing: more demands are made on them by employees, by customers and by government. They are expected to be socially responsible and environmentally concerned, as well as to produce goods and services of higher and higher quality – to avoid losing out to competitors elsewhere, often in countries remote from their own area of immediate operation.

Some organizations will set objectives for themselves which will require close attention to the management of important relationships. A developer, seeking to exploit a site verging on open countryside, may have to negotiate with government at several levels, as well as deal with potential opposition from conservation groups, media and local community groups.

Finally, opportunities and threats which are identified by the organization may require skillful management of relationships. Recently, the company producing Perrier bottled mineral water was threatened by the discovery that its product had been contaminated in production. In a response which involved immediate withdrawal of its product from the market and well-managed reassurances to important groups about the steps being taken to ensure the product's purity, Perrier was able to sustain the company's position and restore the product to the market in a short space of time. The Perrier case is already being cited as a text book example of how a threat to a company should be dealt with, largely because it demonstrates the importance of attending to and managing key relationships at time of threat.

Public relations support is more likely to be needed the more organizations have:

- A turbulent environment
- Pressures they are subject to
- Objectives that require skilful management of important relationships
- Opportunities they can identify which can only be fully realized by careful management of relationships
- Threats that can be identified to their continuing survival and prosperity

Resources available to the organization – internal and external

Resources available to the organization will determine whether or not public relations support can be used and the kind of support that can be obtained. The smaller organization may be pressed to allocate management time to public relations and will do so only if convinced that public relations will make a contribution to overall objectives, such as business growth for a small business, or more effective fund-raising in the case of a charitable organization.

At this stage in the development of public relations practice, there is a general shortage of people recognizably qualified to be effective in public relations roles. More will be said of this shortage in Chapter 11, but it may not be easy for organizations to find the support they are looking for, either through the appointment of qualified personnel, or through services provided by public relations consultancies.

Management and staff attitudes to public relations

It will be easier to argue for the allocation of resources to public relations if managers and staff are prepared to be open-minded about its potential contribution. If public relations is seen as peripheral to the main concerns of management, as a waste of resources, or as an insubstantial and disreputable practice, it will obviously be less easy to convince the organization to make use of public relations.

Experience of public relations

If the organization's experience of public relations has been unsatisfactory in the past, then it will also be difficult to argue that the practice should be taken seriously, and that it does have a contribution to make to the organization and the achievement of its objectives.

Personality of the most senior manager

The comments made about attitudes towards public relations held by other managers and staff apply to the attitudes of the most senior manager, but his or her personality will also affect the likelihood that public relations will be drawn on, and drawn on effectively. If the organization's chief executive is unwilling to play a role in public relations, to represent the organization and to become personally involved in important relationships, for example with the media or with shareholders, then effective use of public relations support may be limited.

The manager deciding upon use of public relations will need to consider options for its management, the environment and pressures facing the organization and the opportunities to be realized if public relations is used well. Organizational resources, staff attitudes and the personality of the most senior manager will also be factors to be weighted into decision-making, as will the threats to the organization from within and outside.

Public relations support will be necessary if:

- The organization has made no provision for managing public relations
- The organization's environment is turbulent and threatening, exerting pressure on the organization but at the same time presenting a number of opportunities

Public relations support will be easier to put into place if:

- The organization has resources it can allocate to, or find for public relations support
- Staff understand public relations' potential contribution or, at least, are open-minded about it
- The organization has had satisfactory experience with public relations support in the past
- The most senior manager understands the potential contribution of public relations and has the personality and inclination to play a role in the organization's public relations activities

Public relations management

Public relations management is concerned with the management of public relations activities. The manager responsible for public relations will need to answer questions such as:

- What public relations activities are required?
- What staff, material and budgetary resources are needed to carry out required activities?
- How can activities be organized into programmes, or specific groups of tasks, and allocated to available staff?

- How can performance be assessed, and public relations activities be monitored and evaluated?

Required public relations activities

Public relations activities are initiated in a number of ways. They may be developed hurriedly in response to a threat or crisis faced by the organization and take the form of a reaction or 'fire-fighting'. The situation largely dictates the public relations activities that will be undertaken, as in the case of a company facing a hostile takeover bid. Public relations activities may also be initiated to capitalize on perceived opportunities. Decisions regarding suitable activities will be made as managers determine the best ways to exploit the opportunities presented.

A more thorough approach to decision-making regarding public relations activities requires a close analysis of the organization's objectives. These will imply supporting public relations objectives, which are the basis for planning programmes of public relations activities. There is a logic to this approach:

Organizational objectives

imply

Supporting public relations objectives

These provide the basis for public
relations programme planning

To take an example: an organization might have, as a broad objective, the intention to reposition itself as a dynamic participant in a developing and competitive market, changing the perceptions held of the organization by employees, competitors, present and potential customers. Implied by this broad objective is the need to work on important relationships, to change perceptions among the groups identified and to change their behaviour towards the organization. Employees might be expected to see the organization in a different way and to change their style of working to demonstrate dynamism and willingness to accept the challenges of operations in a more competitive market.

Organizational objectives imply public relations objectives. Where organizational objectives are not clear, a first step in the development of public relations activities will be to co-operate with management to define them. Here is one of the major values of public relations in management: it can act as a motor for clarifying what the organization is aiming towards. It does this by working to make an organization's objectives clear so that they can be used as a basis for communication with important groups and by providing feedback to the organization on how its objectives are perceived by these groups.

To sum up, required public relations activities will be initiated in response to threats to the organization, in attempts to capitalize on opportunities, or in the course of an analysis of the organization's objectives.

Resources needed

Activities required will suggest the resources needed to carry them out. For example, the large commercial organization faced by a hostile takeover bid will devote considerable resources to a defence against the bid. Sotheby's, threatened by a hostile bid in 1983, was able to mobilise a substantial defence, which included a group of public affairs advisers. They were able to mount a successful lobby of the British government which led to the bid being referred to the Monopolies and Mergers Commission, a government agency which rules on the acceptability of bids. The reference had the effect of stopping the hostile bid. The situation suggested the activities required and the resources needed to carry them out.

Activities will involve an amount of work, which may be sufficient to justify the appointment of internal staff. If the number of activities does not seem to justify an internal appointment, assistance from outside staff resources may be needed: for example, from a public relations consultancy with the staff and expertise to take on the activities identified. Depending on the mix of activities identified, there may be a case for internal and external staff involvement.

Material and budgetary resources will also be determined by the activities required. Resources available will in most cases set limits on the activities which can be undertaken and priorities will have to be set so that the most important activities can be undertaken within the limits of available budgetary resources. We will return to a more detailed discussion of budgeting for public relations activities in Chapter 11.

Organization of activities

Public relations activities are conveniently organized into programmes, series of activities aimed at the achievement of specific objectives. A number of programmes may be the responsibility of one internal staff member, for example all programmes involving work and communication with internal groups. A brief, or set of instructions, to a public relations consultancy may set out objectives to be achieved and ask for recommendations for programmes to achieve them which, if accepted, form the basis for the consultancy's work with the organization.

In a public relations department, staff may be organized according to the programmes the department manages. A department managing relationships with government, the media and the local community might have staff specifically responsible for public affairs, media relations and community relations programmes. Decisions on the arrangements made for work to be carried out will depend on activities required, groups important to the organization, the organization's own structure, resources and the skills of staff available, or likely to be available to the organization.

The terms available to describe public relations activities become especially important when programmes of activity are allocated to staff. Earlier, it was suggested that public relations is an overall term which describes all public relations activities.

Groups of activities can be marked off and described using appropriate terms.

To recap, public relations is that part of the management task concerned with the management of important relationships and with influencing the behaviour of groups which are parties to those relationships. It makes use of managed communication.

Public affairs is a specialist area of practice within public relations. It is concerned with those relationships which are involved in the development of public policy, legislation and regulation, which may affect organizations, their interests and operations. As a specialist area of practice, public affairs attempts to anticipate issues which may arise and to shape their resolution as public policy is developed through public debate and governmental action.

Paraphrasing definitions from the task force document of the Public Relations Society of America[5] mentioned earlier:

Issues management is part of public relations and public affairs practice and involves systematic identification and action regarding public policy matters of concern to an organization

Media relations deals with the communications media in seeking publicity or responding to their interest in the organization

Community relations involves dealing and communicating with citizens and community groups within an organization's operating area

Financial public relations deals with relationships with shareholders of an organization and the investment community

Corporate communications refers to all communications carried on within and by a corporation for corporate purposes. Such communications include publications, such as annual reports, reports to employees, employee newspapers and audio-visual communication techniques used for corporate purposes. Corporate communications techniques are used in public relations practice, but cannot simply be equated with it. Internal communication is an aspect of corporate communication and is also used in public relations, in managing relationships with internal groups

Each of these specialist areas of practice will be covered in coming chapters, but – as the Public Relations Society of America report suggests – 'it is clear from this differentiation that the only term that can provide a suitable "umbrella" is public relations.'

The terms become important in organizing a public relations department, or in assigning work to public relations staff, because each of the terms refers to defined programmes of activity. A public affairs officer, or a public affairs unit within a public relations department, should be mainly concerned with issues management, government relations and monitoring the activities of special interest groups, while a media relations specialist would spend most of his or her time working with organization staff to identify topics of interest to the media, and with journalists. The point to emphasize here is that these terms are not interchangeable but, used accurately, are an aid to public relations management.

Performance assessment and evaluation
Public relations activities can be monitored and evaluated in the same way that other management activities are. Monitoring public relations activities involves assessing progress towards identified objectives, while evaluation is a means of testing whether or not activities undertaken led to the achievement of objectives through appropriate use of time and resources. The key to evaluation in public relations is to set objectives which are specific and which lead, through programmes of activities, to tangible results that can be weighed against the objectives

set. Public relations programmes that are based on objectives to raise awareness, or increase goodwill, will be harder to evaluate than programmes which are aimed at some behavioural results, such as increased support from the general public measured through assessments of letters to local or national newspapers, or attendance at company or organization events.

Public relations as a task of management

In this chapter, public relations has been described as a part of the overall management task. It is still not recognized as an important part of management by many commentators. A survey of management consultancy practice in *The Economist*, published in February 1988,[6] excluded public relations advisers 'since they do not deal with mainstream management problems'. Despite the continuing prevalence of this kind of view, senior managers are now aware of the value of well-managed public relations activities to the success of their organizations.

Public relations builds the relationships which are likely to provide support to organizations as they pursue their objectives. It is an enabling practice, which makes it easier for organizations to pursue their objectives and, at the same time, to take account of the interests of groups involved in those objectives.

As a practice, its aim – and the result on which it should be judged – is to have an effect on behaviour. To influence behaviour, public relations makes use of communication. We will explore the use of communication in public relations practice in the next chapter, which examines media relations as an aspect of public relations.

CHAPTER TWO

MEDIA RELATIONS: COMMUNICATION IN PUBLIC RELATIONS

MEDIA RELATIONS LOOM large in many conceptions of public relations practice. Practitioners in the United Kingdom regularly receive information from organizations offering short training programmes in aspects of public relations which equate successful public relations with getting stories into the media. In some organizations which maintain public affairs, rather than public relations departments, public relations is seen as wholly concerned with media relations.

Historically, public relations emerged from press agentry in the United States. In the early days of public relations practice, publicity was an end in itself, but the practice has moved on and developed, and publicity and media coverage become important now only if the objectives being pursued require them.

In this chapter, we'll consider the role of communication in public relations to show that communication is a tool of public relations, not the sum of the practice. Communication through the media has some obvious advantages, but it is only one of a number of approaches to communication.

Communication in public relations practice

Professor James Grunig, at the University of Maryland in the United States, defines public relations as 'the management of communication between an organization and its publics.'[1] Here, the argument is that public relations is the part of the management task concerned with the management of

23

important relationships, which makes use of communication in trying to influence the ways in which important relationships develop. According to this view, we need to focus first on the groups in relation to each other and their relationships, and *then* on communication as a means of influencing relationships of interest.

As a practice, public relations involves a number of defined phases. As we saw in Chapter 1, public relations activities will be initiated as a response to threats or opportunities or as a result of the analysis of organization objectives. Once initiated, public relations practice includes the following phases:

- *Research*: information is gathered, more or less systematically, and used as a basis for planning programmes of activity
- *Analysis*: information gathered is analysed to plan programmes of activity
- *Action*: plans made are acted upon. This phase of action involves communication (although a decision may be made not to communicate). When it does take place communication is the 'visible' part of public relations practice, and, for many people, constitutes the whole of the practice
- *Evaluation*: in the final phase of public relations practice, activities and results achieved are evaluated against plans. Information derived from evaluation is fed back into planning and decision-making for future activities

Communication is only part of a four-part process. Public relations involves a consideration of situations, possible options, the setting of precise objectives for relationships of importance, the choice of appropriate courses of action (which may involve no communication) and an evaluation of actions taken.

Why then is communication believed to be so important in public relations? It is visible: it is what public relations practitioners seem to do. It is also what public relations practitioners claim to be good at: as Douglas Smith, president of the British Institute of Public Relations in 1990, emphasized in a response to a suggestion that management consultants might move in to the public relations area, 'management consultants, especially the accountancy-based consultancies, are presuming skills they do not possess . . . we are the communication specialists, not management consultants' (*PR Week*, 22 March 1990).

Communication is central to public relations practice, but the skills of research, analysis and evaluation are fundamental, since analysis will suggest courses of action, contents and means of communication and audiences or groups of importance. According to Professor Andrew Kakabadse of Cranfield School of Management, public relations practitioners tend to be tactical in their approach to problem-solving. They tend to suggest solutions to the problems of organizations and their managements in terms of tactics and techniques. Comfortable with techniques, they hurry to recommend their use. This rush to recommend and use techniques has immediate consequences for the quality of advice that practitioners can offer and the kind of advice that managers can expect from public relations advisers.

Techniques of communication in public relations

Communication allows for the exchange of meaning between individuals. It depends on contact between the sender of information and the person who receives the information. In true communication, the receiver can provide feedback to the sender, who can use it to assess the effectiveness of communication. For example, a teacher standing in front of a class can tell immediately from the looks on the faces of members of the class if the point he or she is trying to make is getting across.

Much of what passes for communication in current public relations practice is not communication, since it does not allow for exchange or – unless specific arrangements are made – for receiving and acting upon feedback. The public relations practitioner who prepares a news release for a press conference may not be acting as a communicator, but as someone with some skills in the packaging of information for a narrow purpose. The release by itself is not communication, but it may contribute to communication between the organization and groups important to it.

Communication depends on feedback. Many of the means of passing on information used in public relations – through the media, advertising, direct mail, notice-boards, audio-visual presentations, for example – do not allow for immediate feedback. Special arrangements must be made if feedback is to be gathered. For example, placing a suggestion box by a notice-board may encourage response to notices.

Techniques of communication used in public relations may be mediated or unmediated.

Mediated communication is the form of communication most often associated with public relations practice. It makes use of some medium in order to communicate with individuals or groups of people. For example electronic mail may be used to communicate with an individual, or the mass media to communicate with large groups of people. With mediated communication, special efforts have to be made to gather feedback, to check whether or not intended meanings have been received. As we shall see when we discuss evaluation in more detail in Chapter 10, gathering feedback can be time-consuming and costly, but it is necessary if communication is to take place.

Unmediated communication is face-to-face communication, which is direct between sender and receiver and allows for immediate feedback. It is the most effective form of communication to use where attempts are being made to influence the attitudes and behaviour of others. Studies of the diffusion of innovations in society – the way in which new ideas and products are developed, made available and taken up for use – show that the media and mediated communication alert people to the existence and availability of new products, but that only face-to-face contact with someone whose opinion they trust will persuade them to use or adopt it.

Since public relations aims to influence behaviour, unmediated communication is its more effective tool. However, mediated communication is used to inform, to encourage interest and to raise awareness of organizations and their objectives.

The value of media relations in public relations is best understood in the context of the following factors:

- Communication is only part of the public relations process: the visible, action phase of the process
- Research and analysis precede communication and may dictate that no communication should take place
- Evaluation follows the action phase of public relations, and looks for effects on behaviour
- Of two broad forms of communication – mediated and unmediated – unmediated communication is most effective in achieving the end goals of public relations, those of influencing behaviour. Mediated communication is of value in trying to create awareness and to provide information. Media relations activities are aimed at collaboration with media personnel, so that the channels of communication offered by the media can be made best use of and the widest audience reached

Media relations

Looking back at the network of relationships in which BP carries on its business (Figure 1, page 8) the media are identified as making up a significant group for the company. The media provide information to, and influence other groups – the company itself, government, special interest groups and the general public.

In public relations, the media – newspapers, specialist publications, radio and television – can be regarded in one of two ways:

- As channels of communication, through which information can be passed to reach a wider audience

■ As a group of organizations made up of individuals who have their own interests, but with whom it is possible to co-operate to achieve organizational objectives

Studies of communication reveal that 'gatekeepers' guard the entrance to channels of communication. These gatekeepers make decisions about which information to admit to their channel. Extensive studies have been made about how they make these decisions. Access is granted by persuasion – by presenting information in such a way that the gatekeeper will be able to make a favourable decision easily. Of course, much depends on the manner of persuasion and in practice many journalists, editors and programme makers may object to being viewed solely as gatekeepers to the media.

Public relations practitioners talk of 'selling in' stories to journalists and editors, persuading them of the merits of a particular story and encouraging use of the material they will provide. Material is prepared in a form suitable for use by the media, which explains the widespread use of the news release format to present information – even when the information contained in the release is not news!

The news release is written in a style and according to a format which will make it acceptable in the channels in which it is to be used. It's not an uncommon experience to see a well-written news release, which contains newsworthy information, used verbatim or with minimal editorial changes in newspapers. However, many news releases are poorly written and presented, and simply do not contain news. These releases are a source of irritation and unnecessary work for journalists and editors and do little to contribute to a constructive working relationship between public relations practitioners and journalists.

A good news release should:

■ *Contain genuine news*. Problems of presentation and writing style will be largely overcome if the information is newsworthy

■ *Be prepared in a format which makes it easy to use.* A heading or headline should give an attention-getting summary of the contents of the release. Margins and spacing between lines in the copy should allow for copy editing and the material should be presented on one side of the paper used, so that copy can be typed into whatever systems are used for typesetting without the need for turning pages over

■ *Use a style of writing appropriate for the medium in which the material is to be used.* News style is economic in its use of words and presents the whole story to be told in a sentence – the lead – at the beginning of copy. Points set out in the lead are amplified in the copy which follows. The news release is constructed as a kind of inverted pyramid in which the main points of the story appear at the head of the story, and less important points or points for amplification follow. The inverted pyramid allows stories to be edited from the bottom – less important details can be edited out, but the story remains intact and space is saved

We will come back in a few moments to the question of what constitutes news, but genuinely newsworthy material well presented will be more likely to be received and used by journalists and editors in their gatekeeping role.

Although journalists and others can be seen as gatekeepers, it is more productive in public relations to view them as individuals serving organizations with their own objectives and interests. They also work according to rules which can be understood and accommodated by managers.

Media organizations aim to generate audiences, through providing content of interest to readers or viewers. A test of the value of information to a newspaper or broadcast media outlet is whether or not the information will be of interest to readers or viewers. Editors, journalists and programme makers are in a constant search for information of interest.

Managers, the organizations they work for and public relations practitioners have access to, and a degree of control over information of value to the media. According to the objective they are pursuing it will be of value to them to make information available to the media for their use at certain times. At other times, media interest in the organization and its activities may lead to requests for information. In most cases, there is no reason why information should not be made available. Where information must be restricted, it is quite possible to say so, and to give reasons why information cannot be released in response to a request. Too often, managers resent media interest in their organizations, and believe that a no comment response is a suitable response to media requests for information.

The task in media relations is to work for a coincidence of interests: the journalist or editor needs information, the organization has information at its disposal and specific interests in the way information is to be released. Managers are interested in seeing information released in such a way that the organization's objectives are served. A journalist working for a trade publication might be interested in receiving information and writing about new products as they are made available. An organization which has recently developed a new product might want to see any publicity about the product appear at the time of the product launch. Having information about the product, the organization can decide on the timing of its release and make the information available at a time to suit its objectives for the product.

Journalists and managers' interests can coincide up to a point, but the journalist's obligations are to his or her own organization, its readers or viewers, and to the rules of journalistic practice. The manager's obligations are to his or her organization. A journalist may feel that it is a matter of public interest that details of the inner workings of an organization are reported, but managers in that same organization might feel that investor confidence in the organization might be diminished by publicity given to internal management difficulties. In this case, the journalist's interest will be in disclosure, while the manager's interest will be in withholding information: the two interests are incompatible, but can be discussed – if relationships between managers and journalists are developed, and based on a mutual respect of each other's interests and obligations.

Journalists work according to a set of values and rules, which it is important for managers to know. The rules can also be broken, depending on the journalist with whom the manager may be working and the extent to which he or she feels bound by the rules. Journalistic values include commitments to the public's right to know and to the public interest. Rules will dictate the protection of sources and these will bear on the way information is collected. A manager acting as a source of information needs to establish the rules under which an interview is taking place and should understand that anything that is said may be used, in one way or another. Going on or off the record will determine whether or not information will be attributed to the manager directly, but it will not prevent the information being used. Going off the record should prevent direct attribution of information to the manager as a source.

Too often, managers fail to understand the rules or deal with journalists who may not use information accurately. As a result of these experiences, some managers prefer to have nothing to do with journalists, but opportunities are lost in this approach. Lack of familiarity with the rules under which journalists operate, and poor experiences with journalists can be overcome through regular contact with them. Managers can learn which journalists should be avoided, but the principle of fairness in media relations should still apply to these journalists. This principle is that information available to one journalist should be available to all.

Managing media relations

Some organizations attract more media interest than others. In government, departments involved in controversial areas will come under media scrutiny more frequently than departments concerned with routine administration. In business organizations, media interest will be stimulated by success, dramatic events and situations – by takeover bids, for example, or the interplay of boardroom personalities. Media interest in crisis situations will be immediate and overwhelming, unless the organization is prepared for it. From the organization's perspective, interest in relations with the media will vary according to its objectives, activities and aspirations.

Irrespective, however, of the level of interest on either side, all organizations need to consider the state of their relationships with the media. Media relations also need to be managed: objectives should be set for relations with the media and specific activities should follow from those objectives. Preparation along these lines avoids the problems that can arise if some emergency situation develops which arouses strong media interest. If no preparation has been made, the organization can find itself having to deal with the situation and with learning how to work with journalists.

An excellent case study prepared by Roy Eales[2] on the approach taken by Air Canada to managing its media relations activities illustrates these points.

Air Canada, as a national airline, attracts a great deal of public interest and is prominent in national life. The airline manages media relations in a very proactive way: it anticipates media interest and is organized to respond to it. Line managers at the regional level in Canada are able to speak for the company, having been prepared for their public relations roles and provided with access to position papers which give the company's view. These position papers are prepared by staff of the company's public relations department. The airline tracks media coverage given to the company and manages its public relations activities to address issues which surface in research.

The case study shows how Air Canada has been able to build journalists' understanding of the company over time. This relationship with journalists has been put to the test on a number of occasions, once – embarrassingly for the airline –

when one of Air Canada's planes ran out of fuel half-way across Canada. Because the airline had established its reputation and credibility with journalists as a safe carrier, it was able to ride out its embarrassment and possible damage to its public reputation. Relationships with the media are built before they are needed and can allow for the development of a reservoir of goodwill and understanding which can be drawn on at time of crisis.

The Air Canada case provides one approach to the management of media relations activities. It's a decentralized approach: line managers are able to speak directly to the media with some guidance from a central public relations department. An alternative approach is to restrict media contact to the central department. There are advantages and disadvantages to each of these approaches, which we'll discuss in a few moments.

First we need to consider some of the basics of media relations management. As a specialist area within public relations, media relations work needs to be assigned – to a senior manager if there are no public relations staff in place, or to an appointed public relations staff member or to external consultants. Decisions as to who will speak for the organization have to be made: will the organization be represented by a senior manager, public relations staff or by a number of identified managers? Or will all staff be able to speak to the media, within certain rules? How will consistency of approach be maintained? How will approval be given for staff to speak to the media and who will decide the content of information to be released to the media? What approval procedures will be adopted?

Arrangements have to be made for the staff person responsible for media relations to gather and monitor information about the organization and to assess its value to the media. The person responsible for media relations must have a developed news sense and an ability to see feature article and programme ideas in the work of the organization. These abilities are developed through a close knowledge of media requirements, sometimes acquired through experience as a journalist.

The media relations specialist can gather information about the organization from attendance at management meetings, from internal newsletters and correspondence and from walking about. The effective media relations specialist will work as a kind of journalist-in-residence, finding and developing story ideas from the organization's work. To be effective, the specialist must be trusted and given access to meetings and information.

News from the organization is information that is likely to be of interest to the news media. Other material from the organization may lend itself to feature articles for specialist publications, or to television or radio programmes. When BP recently appointed a new chairman and went through an extensive headquarters reorganization, the changes were sufficiently interesting to merit a lengthy television documentary programme, the BBC's *Money Programme*. News involves novelty, change, drama, a high degree of relevance to the lives of readers and viewers and human interest. The able media relations specialist will understand news and achieve good coverage for the organization – if that is a goal – by identifying items of interest and by making sure that they reach the journalists likely to report them.

Media relations activities have to support the achievement of overall organizational objectives. Publicity – the result of bringing something to public notice – may be courted for its own sake and may be gratifying for those who feature in it, but the most effective kind meets organizational requirements. In other words, the activities that follow from media relations objectives should be evaluated against the overall public relations objectives.

How then do the centralized and decentralized approaches to media relations differ and what are their advantages and disadvantages?

The centralized approach allocates responsibility for media relations to a central point within the organization – only one person, or a small number of people, can speak to the media on the organization's behalf. These individuals may include a senior manager and the head of public relations, or several senior managers, the head of public relations and the media relations specialist. In some organizations, all media enquiries are taken by, and referred to, the head of public relations. In the centralized approach, material for release to the media may have to go through the head of public relations and the organization's senior manager for approval.

The advantage of the centralized approach is that tight control over contact with the media is established and consistency of information released can be checked. Public relations or media relations staff can act as a buffer between the organization and the media and other managers, who may not be willing to deal with the media, can get on with their work without the distraction of media enquiries. The approach is essential at time of crisis, when information must be tightly controlled to avoid confusion and the possibilities of releasing inadequate or contradictory information. During crisis it is also necessary to place a buffer between those seeking information from the organization and the management group who have to deal with the crisis situation.

In situations other than crisis situations, there are a number of disadvantages to the approach. The credibility of the organization is diminished in journalists' eyes, as they are prompted to question why the organization needs to maintain such tight control over information at its disposal. In addition, public relations practitioners lack credibility as sources of information for journalists, particularly when they are perceived to be acting as a buffer between the organization and media personnel.

A further disadvantage of the centralized approach is that it may cause the organization to be slow to respond to even the most simple of information requests. An organization which is dispersed through several regions of a country may be contacted by a journalist working in a regional centre and have to refer the request to central staff. The credibility and sensitivity of the organization in the region are called into question, and the time taken by the organization to respond may render the information provided useless for journalistic purposes.

The decentralized approach avoids some of these disadvantages, but involves others. It allows larger numbers of staff to respond to, and work with, the media. In the Air Canada case, all regional managers were able to respond to media enquiries for information, with guidance from central staff. The decentralized approach depends for its success on preparation of staff for the public relations and media relations aspects of their role: they need training in order to work effectively with the media.

If the decentralized approach is chosen, it's important that clear guidance from central staff is available. Centrally, the organization needs to have in place a policy regarding the release of information by managers to the media. The policy should establish who can say what on the organization's behalf. For an organization with a head office and a number of substantial regional offices, such a policy might specify that the regional senior manager can respond to the media on all matters that affect the organization's regional operations, but that corporate matters involving the whole organization should be dealt with by central office staff. In the decentralized approach, central staff are a resource to regional staff or to line managers, providing information to them in the form of briefing and position papers, as in the Air Canada case.

The disadvantages of the decentralized approach are that control over the flow of information from the organization is lessened, and that it does require a commitment of time and resources to training managers for this aspect of their role. This training is an essential part of training for modern management, but some organizations may not agree, or be willing to commit resources to this training requirement.

Loss of control over information can be serious: one large organization that I worked with as a consultant had recently re-organized to establish a business structure based on business units – divisions of the old organization which were now being allowed a high degree of autonomy. Some months into the reorganization, the company found that its separate business units were making use of their new found freedom to work directly with the media, but providing them with contradictory or confusing information about the company. The confusion created in the minds of members of groups important to the company, such as investment analysts, financial journalists and senior politicians, was causing questions to be raised about the management of the company.

Regardless of the approach to media relations taken, the underlying principles of media relations management are the same:

- Unless there are good reasons for withholding information, arrangements should be made for providing information to the media, at their request or to meet organizational requirements
- These arrangements make up the organization's approach to managing media relations. They involve decisions regarding information and its handling (for example, through policies about information which can be passed to the media, approval processes and designation of personnel who can pass information directly to the media)
- Relationships with journalists, editors and other media personnel should be established and built over time. Journalists' interests and requirements for information should be ascertained and met, as far as this is possible. When it is not possible to meet requirements for information, relationships with journalists and others should be good enough to allow for an honest explanation
- Information provided to journalists and others should be of genuine interest to them – it should be newsworthy, or fit the needs of the publications or programmes for which they work

Managing   media   relations   requires   an   allocation   of managerial time to the task. The scale of the task will be determined by the organization's objectives and the situations in which the organization finds itself. An organization aggressively seeking to expand may need to generate media coverage of its activities to support its objectives. Similarly, an organization forced by economic circumstances to contract will have to explain how contraction will affect its long-term prospects as a business.

The task of media relations may be delegated, as we have seen, to a central staff group or individual, or − with rules established throughout the organization − to individuals at all levels of the organization. In a large central staff group, relations with various media − print, specialist or broadcast − may be allocated to individual staff members. More often, though, one individual will deal with all media.

Good relations with the media are essential − not so that the organization can guarantee for itself good and favourable coverage, or good publicity − which it can't − but so that lines of communication are open. The value of openness is particularly apparent at times of crisis, but its benefits are also realized whenever the organization's activities are called into question. Where relationships are already established and the organization is known to journalists, members of the organization know who they can contact to explain their objectives and activities. Favourable coverage cannot be guaranteed, but having relationships with the media already in place will improve the likelihood that coverage will be informed.

CHAPTER THREE

INTERNAL GROUPS: PUBLIC RELATIONS AND ITS ROLE WITHIN THE ORGANIZATION

AMONG THE GROUPS that are most important to any organization are those which make up the organization: its own staff and employees. A number of established functions in the human resource management, personnel or industrial relations areas will claim strong interests in the health of relations with these groups, but it is only recently that public relations practitioners have asserted their role in helping to manage relations with internal groups. In Britain, for example, the national Institute of Personnel Management examined the possibilities for collaboration between personnel departments and public relations practitioners in 1989, in a book entitled *The Communications Challenge: Personnel and PR Perspectives*, compiled by personnel specialists and public relations practitioners.[1]

The public relations perspective on the internal 'public' sees the members of an organization as a group of people whose perceptions of the organization cannot be left to develop accidentally. Organizations depend on the support of the people who make them up, if they are to achieve their objectives efficiently, and withstand competition or other external threats. From a public relations perspective, the people who make up an organization are also its representatives: their behaviour, what they say about the organization to others and their unstated attitudes to the organization, all reflect on it.

Support for the organization has to be won and re-won, but there is a more fundamental point to be made. Organizations are imaginary creations – they are created in the minds of the people who make them up. New employees are inducted into organizations and have to learn what they are about, and what is important about the organizations they are joining. The beliefs held by employees about the organizations they are part of are established over time – and can be changed.

A major task for managers is to manage 'meaning' within organizations. This is not an abstract point: it means that managers have to point out, to the people making up the organization, what is significant and important in their membership of that organization. This is another argument for clear communication by managers, but communication which goes beyond the written or spoken word to include symbols and details of the working environment, such as signage and interior design.

An excellent example of communication with internal groups is found in the work of the Prudential Corporation,[2] which recently changed its corporate identity to reflect changes it had undergone and to facilitate future change. The company hoped to alert important groups, such as the investment community, the general public and its own staff to the company's dynamism and ability to compete in the rapidly changing financial services market. The company launched its new corporate identity in September, 1986, in a move which attracted more press publicity for the company than any other event in its 140-year history. The move was seen as confirmation of the company's intent to realize its potentital as a leading financial services provider. Within the company, the new image had a powerful – and intended – impact on Prudential staff. The new look served to focus attention and reaffirm a common purpose and identity for the corporation.

David Vevers, then manager of public affairs for the corporation, said that preparation for the development of the new identity was the first time that management had really considered how it communicated internally and externally. 'The Prudential had under-estimated the need for a unified image that correctly portrayed the underlying spirit of the company. Our name was strong and yet it did not appear in any consistent way in the identities created by the operating companies. As a result, our customers, and even many of our own staff, didn't fully understand what the Prudential stood for,' says Vevers. 'We started a process of looking at all the identities used within the corporation. We listed all their different names and those of the products to see how they realted. In reality, we found that they didn't.'

A number of objectives were set for the identity programme. It had to bring together all companies within the group under a common banner and in a way which was appropriate to the Prudential's development as a major financial services provider – not just an insurance company. It also had to be flexible enough to be used across the company's services, and it had to be distinctive.

The design solution for these objectives brought together two key strengths – the Prudential's name and what it embodied. Prudence – represented in the new identity (Figure 2) – incorporated the very principles the corporation stands for – wise conduct.

Figure 2 The Prudential symbol

The new identity was launched to about a third of the Prudential's staff in the United Kingdom, in 12 one-hour presentations held in London in September, 1986, for all managers in the company and a cross section of other staff. The presentations explained the changes facing the company and the rationale behind the new corporate identity, and made effective use of communication technology, such as video, to create a strongly motivational occasion for staff. According to David Vevers, 'the identity programme was 80 per cent targeted at staff.' It was intended to motivate, and to change the way staff felt about the company and, he felt, it worked.

The Prudential case demonstrates how symbols and core values within an organization are used in communication with internal groups and to influence and manage the relationship between organization and its own members.

Management of internal communication programmes

The senior manager considering the relationship between the organization and its own members, and how this can be influenced and managed, will need to take into account:

- Formal agreements which may exist between the organization, its employees and, perhaps union groups, such as contracts and agreements on working conditions. These agreements will be of special interest to personnel departments and industrial relations specialists
- The organization: its values and the way in which its values affect the organization's approaches to its activities. For example, does the organization have a mission statement which guides its behaviour towards customers or employees, or a code of conduct which governs the behaviour of members of the organization?
- The organization's objectives: do these explicitly require the support of employees? If so, how will support be ensured?

- The current state of the relationship between the organization and its employees
- Whether there is a need for change in the relationship between the organization and its employees.
- If there is a need for change, how can it be brought about, and what part should communication play in bringing about change?
- If communication is to play a part in bringing about change, what effects will be sought from the use of communication, what form should it take and what should its content be?
- If programmes of communication are required, how should it be managed, and by whom?

What is looked for in the organization's relationship with its employees is support that goes beyond the legal requirements of a contract of employment. The ideal is willing, highly motivated support for the organization and its objectives. Such support is won through honest communication in which reasons for support are set out. It needs to be stressed that what is being talked about here is not a form of manipulation, but an approach which recognizes the legitimate interests of the organization and the people who make it up, and tries to reconcile them, in communication which is aimed at winning support for the organization and its objectives.

This ideal is put to practical test at times of difficulty for the organization. A good example is to be found when organizations have to contract, and to lay off employees. The experience of Dow Chemical Canada in closing a small manufacturing plant in western Canada demonstrates how communication can be used to sustain the support of employees and the local community through difficult circumstances. The plant facility in British Columbia which produced benzoic acid and phenol had been running at a loss for several years before the company decided to close it. Although it employed only 36 people, the company made well-planned provision for the employees who were to be made redundant. It also planned to communicate with local community leaders and media, so that they would have a full understanding of the reasons for the closure of the plant.

Senior managers from Dow Canada – including the company's western region public relations director – were involved in the announcement of the closure to employees, who were given generous severance payments and assistance with their search for other employment. Because of the sympathetic approach taken by the company to its employees' requirements for information and assistance, the closure was effected without damage to the company's reputation in the local community and without disruption to relations with other employees retained by the company. The small number of employees who were made redundant were reported to be satisfied with the treatment and help given to them by the company.

The case, written up in the *Public Relations News*,[3] a newsletter for public relations practitioners published in the United States, shows how a major company – Dow Chemical Co. of Midland, Michigan, which employed over 54,000 people in 28 countries at the time of the closure – can attend to the details of communication with employees who represent only a fraction of its workforce and take their interests into account, reconciling them with organizational interests and objectives.

Willingness to recognize the legitimate interests of employees and to try to communicate honestly with them in order to reduce the possibilities of misunderstanding and conflict is a basic value in organizational life.

Management writers such as Robert Blake and Jane Mouton[4] have suggested that managers can be distinguished by examining their concern for the people who work with them and their concern for the tasks in hand. The manager oriented towards production, the task in hand, will be less inclined to spend as much time on attending to the needs and interests of employees than the manager whose orientation is towards people and to motivating them to be productive. The approach we are discussing here makes the assumption that people will be more likely to be motivated to work, and to give active support to the organizations employing them, if their interests are recognized and they are provided with the information they need to be effective.

The support needed from employees will be clear from an examination of the organization's objectives. An organization faced with the immediate problems of surviving difficult market conditions will need understanding from employees, particularly if redundancies are in prospect. The organization will still depend on the employees who remain to see it through short-term difficulties – their motivation will need to be maintained even though they see colleagues losing their positions. The objectives of survival and maintenance of employee morale will require that the organization explain the situation it is facing to its employees. Similarly, an organization intending to expand will need to inform its employees about the demands that will be made upon them and the rewards likely to follow from expansion.

Communication takes place in organizations in both formal and informal ways. The internal structure of an organization and its hierarchy will give rise to the formation of certain relationships between employees. These will include inter-departmental relationships – for example, between sales and marketing departments – and those between a manager and the people reporting to him or her. Within the structure will be other relationships formed because people – either indi-vidually or in groups – naturally make decisions about whom they want to work with and whom they will befriend. A manager intending to take a more systematic approach to communication within an organization will need, in addition to an appreciation of the organization's values and objectives, an insight into the existing state of relationships in the organization.

This insight can be intuitive, based on what the manager knows about the organization, or it can be derived from a communications audit, an approach to finding out about relationships in the organization which is based on research.

The communications audit, developed in studies of personnel management in the 1950s, is a broad scale, loosely structured research exercise, which examines the effectiveness of communication within organizations and between organizations and groups outside. Internally, the communications audit uses a survey approach to find out how well the organization is communicating with its own members: do they understand the organization's objectives, and their role in helping the organization to achieve its objectives? How well do they feel the organization communicates its objectives to them and how could communication within the organization be improved?

The need for a communications audit will be prompted by the arrival of a new manager who needs to understand how well the organization is communicating with its own members, or by problems in the organization – such as high turnover of staff or high rates of absenteeism – which suggest that communication is not taking place. A decision to undertake an audit is not without risk, since the activities of asking staff how communication can be improved will raise expectations that improvements will follow. Managers thinking of carrying out an audit must be prepared for the possibility that the audit will indicate the need for changes, which they must be willing to undertake to make if necessary. Failure to act on the findings of an audit, where the need for change is made obvious, will damage the credibility of management and may exacerbate the situation the audit was intended to uncover and relieve.

An audit may also be necessary when existing communication programmes – involving employee newsletters and other forms of systematic communication with employees, for example – have been in place for some time and their effectiveness needs to be checked.

The manager's own judgement and intuitition, and the results of any audit which may be carried out, will indicate the state of relationships within the organization, and whether or not improvements are needed in the approaches taken to communication. If improvements are indicated, the manager will need to ask what specific effects are to be sought from improved communication. These might include:

- A measurable improvement in employee morale, which might be seen in diminished levels of absenteeism, lower staff turnover, or more favourable attitudes to the organization measured in follow-up surveys
- Improved understanding of the organization and its objectives assessed intuitively or through follow-up survey work
- A reduction in conflict between groups making up the organization
- Higher levels of productivity and motivation

To try to achieve these changes, the manager is faced with the tasks of deciding on the form communication should take, and its content. Communication, as we saw earlier (Chapter 2), can be direct and face-to-face, or mediated in some way. Face-to-face communication is the basis of management. The most authoritative studies of the way managers actually work have demonstrated the extent to which managers depend on face-to-face communication to be effective. Much of this direct face-to-face communication is informal – spontaneous and unplanned – but it can also be systematic, carried on in specially held meetings, or conducted through presentations and briefing sessions. Face-to-face communication will be more persuasive and motivating and more likely to have an impact on attitudes and behaviour.

Mediated communication for internal purposes may make use of special publications, such as employee newsletters or newspapers, or reports to employees. It may also use audio-visual techniques, video or slide presentations, telephone news or information lines, or electronic mail. Suggestion schemes remove the need for face-to-face communication, by establishing systems which can be used by employees to communicate indirectly with management, to make suggestions or, in some cases, to ask questions about management policies, intentions and actions.

The content of communication will be dictated by objectives to be pursued, the effects sought, the means of communications chosen and the needs and interests of the groups involved. An organization setting out with the objective of improving communication with its members and intending to raise their awareness of its activities might choose to prepare a report to employees. This might be modelled on a report to shareholders, but prepared in shortened form without details required by shareholders, for employees and their families. The choice of a report, to be written in readable and interesting style, would lead to certain design considerations and the use of illustrations to create interest. Employees' needs would be for a publication that would provide them with information of real interest.

Managing internal communication

How should internal communication be managed, and who should have responsibility for the management of communication within organizations? Clearly, all managers have a role in internal communication, as do all employees. Organizations depend on communication for their existence, since it enables people, as individuals and in groups, to work together. Much of this communication is informal and spontaneous, but some depends on the organization's structure, which determines some relationships – such as reporting relationships – and the communication that can take place within them.

Some internal communication can be managed. Managers at the head of the organization can plan and put into place programmes of communication aimed at groups within the organization. A marketing director, for example, might devise a programme using a newsletter and other publications to keep sales staff informed of new product developments; or senior management may decide upon a systematic briefing programme, cascading down through the organization to keep all staff informed of management intentions.

Responsibility for programmes of internal communication

remains with senior management, but this may be delegated to public relations, personnel or other staff, such as regional managers. Some problems may arise here if responsibilities for internal communication are not defined clearly. Personnel and public relations staff have interests in internal communication, but from different perspectives. Possibilities for collaboration or conflict exist – as *The Communications Challenge*[5] suggests: 'In normal times, the different aspects of the personnel and PR role sometimes lead to overlap and confusion . . . in times of crisis, caused by strikes, accidents or commercial upheavals, the co-ordination of the two specialist roles is put to the severest test . . . it is then that the strengths and weaknesses of the organization's policy and strategy on communications are revealed in action.'

The approach to be taken to internal communication needs to be thought out as management tasks are considered and allocated. If responsibility for internal communication is retained by senior management, as it obviously will be in a small business, then it will be important for senior managers to consider their attitudes towards communication with employees and to give time and attention to this task.

In larger organizations, responsibilities for internal communication will need to be assigned clearly. One possible assignment of responsibility might involve staff in the personnel department having a lead role in determining internal communication tasks to be carried out, with the public relations department providing advice and technical services. In another possible arrangement, senior management might agree with the heads of personnel and public relations functions how the two departments are to collaborate to achieve organization goals, or to assist the organization to face specific situations, such as strikes or extended industrial disputes.

Arrangements made will need to fit the organization's requirements and resources. An organization headed by a group of managers who regard the task of communicating well with its members as important, who have the resources and a well-developed sense of how communication is to be managed on the organization's behalf, may have a public relations department that contains specialists in internal communication. An organization in which senior management has decided that costs involved in supporting staff departments, such as personnel and public relations, are to be held to a minimum, may opt for a leaner approach, in which internal communications are managed by a personnel specialist, drawing on technical assistance from external public relations consultants.

Internal communications programmes may involve these elements:

- *Research among internal groups*, to establish the need for communication and approaches to be taken, and to monitor the effectiveness of communication
- *Specific communication techniques*, aimed at producing desired effects in the pursuit of identified objectives. For example, the introduction of a company newspaper to keep employees informed about developments within the company

They may be managed by a member of senior management, or by identified specialist staff, in personnel or public relations departments.

Techniques and tools of internal communication

Programme development in internal communication will involve choices from a wide variety of communication techniques and tools. Internal communication can involve:

Interpersonal communication
- *Face-to-face meetings or briefings*. These can be conducted through a system of 'cascade' briefing, which allows for information to be cascaded down through the organization via meetings between supervisors and their staff. Another systematic approach may involve a series of visits, by senior managers, to staff at various locations in which

the organization operates, so that staff can be brought up-to-date on developments in the organization. These visits enable senior managers to gather information on staff concerns throughout the organization

- *Training.* Training can be used for the purposes of organization development, to help meet objectives for customer service or other organizational objectives, as well as to meet the personal development needs of staff. Most forms of training involve face-to-face communication between instructor and trainer or staff, but there are hundreds of approaches to staff and management development to choose from (see, for example, the *Encyclopedia of Management Development Methods*, by Andrzej Huczynski[6])

Mediated communication

- *Written communication.* Written communication used for internal purposes includes memos, letters and notices. As with other forms of communication used by management, these are often left unexamined. It's often a useful exercise to check internal memos for style, tone and readability. There are a number of tests for the readability of written material, which involve checks on sentence length and counts of the number of long words. Longer sentences and excessive use of long words will make copy more difficult to read

- *Publications.* Publications used for the purposes of internal communication include manuals – setting out policies and procedures – and publications such as reports to employees or internal newsletters, newspapers and magazines. These publications have to strike a difficult balance between serving management objectives and meeting staff requirements for information that is complete and interesting. Publications that fail to strike this balance may be dismissed by employees as a form of management propaganda, or viewed by insecure management as being too open with information about the organization and its operations. Successful publications can serve management objectives, by making a genuine contribution to under-standing of the organization and its objectives, and satisfy staff needs for information. Modern production techni-ques and use of design can make internal publications extremely attractive and interesting to read. Skilful edit-ing, by staff who know the organization and its politics and who have good journalistic skills, makes a major contribu-tion to the effectiveness of internal publications

- *Audio-visual techniques,* including use of slide-tape presenta-tions and videos, are relatively recent additions to the range of techniques available for use in internal communi-cation. They allow for the dramatic and vivid presentation of information about the organization, but are difficult to use well. If used excessively, or inappropriately, these techniques may irritate

- *Telephone information or news lines.* Used by some large organizations, telephone news lines involve the regular recording of news and information, available to members of the organization via a central telephone number. Telephone news lines allow for quick transmission of current information, but employees may choose not to make use of the service they provide

- *Electronic mail.* This can be used for much the same purposes as telephone news lines. It can make the same information available to all members of the organization who have access to systems. In the Air Canada case looked at earlier (Chapter 3), company position statements were made available to all regional managers by electronic mail, so that when questioned by the media, they were able to call these statements up and use them as a basis for their response

- *Suggestion schemes* break into face-to-face communication by allowing for anonymous written communication between staff and management, which passes through some intermediary. These schemes may allow for sugges-tions to be made which will improve practices within the organization. More elaborate schemes may allow employees to pose questions to management and receive answers: questions pass to an intermediary – a member of staff in a personnel department charged with running the scheme, for example – who detaches the name of the questioner from the question and passes it on to management for an answer. When the answer is received it is sent on, by the intermediary, to the person who asked the question. These schemes require management commitment and need to be properly introduced and explained. If effective, they can provide another channel of communication within the organization

It is impossible and unwise to ignore the importance of the grapevine, the informal communication that takes place in organizations between their members. Many studies of communication in organizations have demonstrated the importance of the grapevine for employees as a source of information. As Roger Feather suggests, in *Inside Organizational Communication*,[7] a book prepared by the International Association of Business Communicators: 'Many managements abhor the grapevine, but it is a normal, natural information channel in all organizations.' He suggests that managers should accept and work with the grapevine, rather than treat it as an undesirable feature of organizational life.

Summary points

In this chapter, we've considered the importance of the internal public and the need to manage the relationship between the organization and its own members. This is a task of public relations, but it is one that is shared with other groups, in particular with staff working in personnel areas. Managers faced with the task of managing internal relationships need to give adequate attention to it and draw on help from specialists in personnel management and public relations when necessary. Public relations staff should have a ready grasp of available techniques for internal communication and be able to advise on the most appropriate approaches to internal communication. These may include elements involving face-to-face communication, skilled and sympathetic use of the organizational grapevine, written and audio-visual communication. In all efforts of internal communication, it is important to remain aware of the objectives being worked towards and the effects desired from communication.

CHAPTER FOUR

PUBLIC AFFAIRS

AS WE SAW in Chapter 1, public affairs is a specialist area of practice within public relations. It is concerned with those relationships that are involved in the development of public policy, legislation and regulation, and which may affect organizations, their interests and operations. As a specialist area of practice, public affairs attempts to anticipate issues that may arise and to shape their resolution as public policy is developed through public debate and governmental action.

Many practitioners who carry the title of public affairs will argue strongly against the inclusion of public affairs under the broad heading of public relations. They will do so for some of the following reasons:

- Common usage and misconceptions of the term public relations suggest a practice which is superficial and dubious. If public relations is conceived of as mainly concerned with publicity and media relations, then it is clear that public affairs is a quite different practice. It involves social and political analysis and judgements as to when organizations should intervene – in public debate, or in the activities of governments or special interest groups – to pursue their interests. If the broader view of public relations put forward in this book is held, then public affairs fits quite comfortably as a specialist area of practice within it

- A desire to avoid association with the title of public relations. Public affairs is often used as an alternative title to public relations for public relations practitioners. An examination of the responsibilities of individuals carrying the title of public affairs will often reveal that the duties to be carried out are indistinguishable from those of public relations practitioners

- A wish on the part of public affairs practitioners to present the practice in which they are involved as more intellectually demanding and worthy of respect than 'mere' public relations. Public relations, based on skills in social analysis, knowledge of its place in management and well-developed knowledge of, and skills in, effective intervention in social situations, is a demanding practice. The skills of the public relations practitioner are augmented in public affairs practice by knowledge of the processes by which public policy emerges from public debate and government decision-making

The argument between public relations and public affairs practitioners about the merits of their activities will continue for some time, and is a feature of the relatively recent emergence of public relations as a part of the overall management task. For the manager, trying to decide whether or not the organization needs a public relations or public affairs practitioner to help it achieve its objectives, the argument is largely academic and is, in the end, between generalists and specialists working in the same broad area of management.

Public affairs practice

Skilled public affairs practitioners are familiar with the workings of government, at political and administrative levels, and know how civil servants and politicians relate, as they work to respond to public issues and interests, social needs and political imperatives. They also appreciate how issues – matters of concern to the public or to special interest groups – emerge, come to provide a focus for public debate and political action, and move through public debate and political action to be resolved, possibly through government regulation or legislation.

This specialized knowledge is added to the skills of the public relations practitioner, which include research, communication and intervention skills. Intervention skills are the skills involved in acting in social situations to bring about some desired change. For example, the skilled public affairs practitioner knows when to intervene with civil servants and politicians as a matter comes to be discussed within government departments and at the political level. As a general rule, intervention should come earlier rather than later, but the able practitioner will also be able to intervene at a late stage in discussion of some public issue with some hope of success. The Sotheby's case, mentioned briefly in Chapter 1, is a good example of how skilled public affairs practitioners can act to influence government.

Another good example is to be found in the programme developed for the Tobacco Alliance by Daniel J. Edelman Limited in 1987 to influence the decisions made by the British Chancellor of the Exchequer regarding taxation of tobacco in the 1987 budget.[1] The programme was devised for the Tobacco Alliance, established some years earlier to act as a communications network for organizations and groups having an interest in the tobacco industry. A major theme for the Tobacco Alliance is putting the case for fair treatment on tobacco tax and arguments were developed in the approach to the 1987 budget for a freeze on tobacco tax.

In a summary of the programme prepared for submission to the British Institute of Public Relations' annual award competition (in which Edelman won an award for best public affairs programme), a number of clear objectives were identified for the public affairs programme. It was to argue in favour of a tax freeze, using strong factual arguments, and to generate extensive media coverage.

The programme was distinguished by the way in which the Alliance presented its arguments, drawing in tobacco retailers to make the case for a freeze to individual Members of

Parliament. In all, 250 members were to receive documents setting out the case for a freeze. They were chosen because of constituency tobacco interest, rank, committee memberships, or electoral vulnerability. Contact was made with MPs through constituency activity and through a lobby of MPs at the House of Commons, but this contact was carefully controlled and used to generate media coverage.

In the 1987 budget no extra tax was imposed on tobacco, and the consultancy was confident that the programme devised had reached its objectives. In particular, the programme resulted in media coverage which the consultancy felt was factual and sympathetic.

The use of public affairs techniques to support the interests of the tobacco industry raises some important ethical questions, which we will return to in the next chapter, but the Tobacco Alliance case illustrates public affairs as it is practised. Practice depends on the same approach to objective setting and planning found in other public relations work, but it is focussed on the resolution of an issue which is in the public domain and which can be resolved through discussion with the groups that have an interest in its resolution. In the Tobacco Alliance's case, the issue was the tax treatment of tobacco, and the effect of taxation levels on the interests of the tobacco industry. The Alliance's arguments were for a freeze on taxation on tobacco. Ranged against the Alliance were all those groups having an interest in raising the level of taxation: the government and special interest groups concerned with smoking and health and the use of taxation as a means of discouraging the consumption of tobacco products.

As in general public relations practice, the objectives of the Alliance were pursued in the context of the relationships important to the Alliance: the government, special interest groups (supporters and opponents) and the media. What distinguishes specialist public affairs practice from public relations practice is its focus on issues and the interest that it has in political processes and in particular with groups such as politicians, civil servants and interest groups.

We'll look at some of these features of public affairs practice before going on to consider management approaches to public affairs: when is it necessary for an organization to become involved in public affairs activities and how should they be managed?

Issues management

Within public relations and public affairs practice, issues management involves systematically identifying issues which may arise and have an impact on an organization's ability to operate.[2] Action is then taken to shape public debate on those issues and to have an impact on the development of public policy in relation to them. Issues, broadly, are all matters of public concern – potential or actual.

Issues can be identified using a number of techniques. An organization may use its own management groups to identify issues facing it, asking them at regular intervals to list and attach priority to the issues they identify. A brewing company operating in several countries may define changing public attitudes to the consumption of alcohol in one country as evidence of an 'issue'.

Another approach depends on scanning the organization's environment to identify early warning signals that issues are about to arise. These signals may be found in economic indicators, in specialist publications or even in the mass media.

Examinations of the content of the mass media will provide indications of trends in coverage of topics and issues of public interest. Issues current in the British mass media as this is written include the safety of transportation systems, the treatment of animals reared for food and the state and capacity of the country's prison system. A company providing transportation services would need to attend to the progress of public debate on the issue of transportation safety, since it is likely to lead on to increased government regulation to ensure that safety standards are set and followed. A construction company interested in the possibility of work on the building of new prisons might follow the public debate on prison capacity with close attention.

A number of companies provide media monitoring services which identify trends and issues surfacing in media coverage.

Another approach to identifying issues is the Delphi approach. This identifies a group of experts and asks for their opinion regarding emerging issues, through a number of rounds of questioning. Organizations may also develop pictures of the future for themselves by creating scenarios, projecting a limited number of trends into the future. At present, many organizations are asking themselves how they will be able to recruit sufficient numbers of younger employees, since the numbers of young people available for employment will decline in the next few years. A picture of the future which suggests smaller numbers of available young people also suggests that the organization contemplating such a future should look to other groups for the staff they will need.

The Delphi approach may use survey techniques to gather responses from the group of experts chosen. In the first round of questioning, the experts will be asked a number of questions about their views of the future and issues likely to be important. In the second round, the views gathered in the first are passed back to the group for comments and additions. The approach can continue until no new information is gathered and a degree of consensus has been reached.

Public affairs practice makes use of research and survey techniques, such as the Delphi approach, not only to identify issues but also to track their development. One method is to use public opinion research.

Once identified, issues need to be monitored, so that organizations can decide how to act to have an impact on the progress of issues into public debate. A major emphasis in public affairs practice is that it is proactive, not reactive, meaning that it prompts initiative rather than reaction: organizations can, if they are sufficiently well informed, act to shape the progress and resolution of an issue in public debate.

Action, as we saw in the Tobacco Alliance case, may involve the public presentation of arguments, and direct work with special interest groups, the media and government. Studies of the way in which issues develop show that, at an early stage in the development, they are adopted by interest groups who, because they can be single-minded in their championing of an issue, can be very effective in winning public and media support for their position.

Political processes, politicians, civil servants and interest groups

Public affairs practice depends on political realism and on an appreciation of how power and influence are used in order to achieve identified objectives. In any particular national society, the public affairs practitioner needs an understanding of how political processes unfold, how politicians are elected and can be reached and how, within the government's administrative machinery, legislation and regulations are brought forward for political debate and approval.

In Europe, it is increasingly important for practitioners to have a knowledge of European institutions, such as the European Commission in Brussels and the European Parliament in Strasbourg.

To a very limited extent, knowledge and understanding of the composition of national and other governmental bodies can be derived from directories which give details of government departments and personnel. Effectiveness in the public affairs role comes from personal and direct knowledge of the processes of politics and the personalities already involved and likely to become involved in the future. Some of the most effective public affairs practitioners are people who have themselves been active in politics at some time in their careers.

Relationships with politicians and with officials should be established routinely, so that they are in place when needed. This is the same principle that we saw at work in media relations (Chapter 2) – relationships are developed before they are needed, not at the time of need.

Public affairs practitioners also need to be familiar with interest groups involved in issues of concern – who are their leaders, how are they structured, what is their ideology, where does their support come from, how are they effective? It will be important to know the personalities involved and the extent to which the interest groups are willing to use conflict and confrontation as means of pursuing their goals. This information forms the basis of 'intelligence' about interest groups, and can be used to work with, against or in spite of them.

Public affairs, because of the information gathered in scanning and monitoring activities, and because of its potential to gather useful information about the intentions of government and special interest groups, is an important source of intelligence. This can be – and should be – fed in to strategic planning and senior management decision-making within the organization.

Decisions on public affairs management

Public affairs is a part of public relations, which in turn is part of the overall management task. It does require allocation of managerial or other staff time, and resources. It is, for example, time-consuming to make contact with local politicians, or with civil servants in relevant departments, and this time may not be made available if there is no immediate benefit to be derived from the contacts. Even so, the smallest organization does need to consider its relationships with local government officials – for example, the small business which may foresee asking for planning permission to extend its premises – and to be alert to issues that may arise to disrupt its activities.

Some of the questions facing managers considering whether or not to allocate time and resources to public affairs activities are:

■   How informed do they need to be regarding the intentions of government in areas of concern to their organizations?

■ How important is it that they keep abreast of social, economic and political issues that may have an impact on the operations of their organizations?

■ Do they have sufficient information, for planning purposes, regarding the intentions of government or special interest groups?

■ Would they be able to respond to government plans for unfavourable legislation or regulation?

■ Could they anticipate, and act to head off, action by special interest groups, which might have negative effects on their organizations?

If answers to these questions suggest that work does need to be done in the public affairs area, a number of decisions could follow. Managers in small organizations might decide to allocate some management time to public affairs, making arrangements to meet systematically with local government officials and politicians and relying on trade and business associations to keep them up-to-date on the development of issues of importance. Managers in larger organizations may pass the tasks involved in public affairs to specialist staff, allowing research and library staff to carry out the tasks of scanning and monitoring the external environment and specialist publications. This would be done under the supervision of public affairs staff, who would also have responsibility for making contact with government officials, politicians and special interest groups.

A number of possible arrangements are found in practice. The tasks of public affairs my be given to a public affairs department, in which public relations is relegated to the media relations and publicity tasks mentioned earlier. Alternatively, public affairs may be a specialist area within a broadly conceived public relations department, which is concerned with all important relationships, allocating relationships with government to specialist public affairs staff. Within public relations consultancies – for example, the large Charles Barker group of consultancies in the United Kingdom – a specialist group may work on public affairs and government relations activities.

Another arrangement for managing public affairs activities in large companies involves the appointment of issue specialists. These are public affairs or other staff who are asked to become familiar with complex issues which will have a major impact on the organization and to guide the organization's response to those issues. Current examples of issues for companies operating in Europe are the changes associated with the move to a single market and all facets of current concern for the environment.

Specialist help from outside the organization is especially valuable in public affairs practice. A consultancy focussed on public affairs practice is able to establish the contacts needed for effective public affairs activity, as well as to maintain offices or links in government centres such as Brussels, Washington and London. The principals of public affairs consultancies will be likely to have very good personal contacts with senior politicians and civil servants.

Lists of consultancies and the services they provide are available from organizations such as the Public Relations Consultants Association[3] in the United Kingdom, or through directories such as the *Hollis Press and Public Relations Annual*.[4] This annual is an invaluable guide to all aspects of public relations practice in the United Kingdom, Europe and elsewhere and is a starting point for any enquiry about public relations and public affairs services.

Summary points

Public affairs practice is concerned with the political aspect of public relations practice, and constitutes a specialist practice within the broad practice of public relations. There will be a disagreement among practitioners on this last point, but for the manager this disagreement should not obscure the requirements of the organization and how they can be met. Public affairs work will be necessary when it is clear that the organization needs to attend to issues within its social environment and to ensure that its point of view and interests are understood and acted upon sympathetically by government. Public affairs work will also be necessary if the organization is the subject of interest group or – in a term current in north American usage – activist group attention.

Options for managing public affairs activities include allocating management time to the tasks involved, such as contact with government officials, or allocating the tasks to specialist staff within or outside the organization. External advisers are particularly valuable because of their knowledge of techniques and contacts.

CHAPTER FIVE

COMMUNITY RELATIONS

ONE WAY OF differentiating specialist practices within the broad sweep of public relations practice is to do so on the basis of the publics or groups of main concern. Media relations is mainly concerned with relations with the media; investor relations' focus is on relations with investors; government relations deals with relations with government and so on.

Community relations is an area of public relations practice that incorporates relations with the community of which the organization is part. Community may refer to the local community, immediately around a factory, for example, or it may refer to the national community. A company may try to demonstrate that it is a good corporate citizen of the larger national community by supporting a programme of sponsorship of the arts.

Why should community relations be marked out for special attention? There are some obvious answers to this question, but we need to look at it against the interests of local, national and – now – international communities. At the local level, a company operating a factory in a small town will need to consider relations with the local community which will be a source of employees and support for company activities. Support can easily be withdrawn and has to be earned and sustained. At the national level, a company operating from a base in a foreign country may need to earn public approval of its activities from the national community. An example of this is to be found in the experience of United States-based multinational companies operating in Europe: these companies have to work constantly to demonstrate their 'European' credentials in the approach to the single market in the European Economic Community.

Because of developments like the move to a single market in western Europe, it is now possible to think in terms of an international community to which companies and other organizations have to relate. Airlines, for example, now have to think of relating to an international travelling public. Similarly, companies such as the luxury goods company Dunhill, recognize that their products and services are consumed world-wide and that their relationships are with groups of people dispersed around the world.

For managers, there are two ways of looking at community relations. Community relations can be viewed as a means to an end: at the local level, a company may recognize that it will need to establish good relations with schools and youth organizations as a means of raising awareness among young people of the company as a potential employer. Community relations activities are undertaken because they will directly serve the company's need for a supply of employees from among the young people in the local community.

The second way of looking at community relations goes beyond the first to ask: what are the obligations of the company to the community or communities in which it operates? How can these obligations be met and bring benefits to the company and to the community? Which community relations activities will do most to help the company to achieve its objectives and to benefit the community?

Some obligations to the community are defined in law. In most countries, the law will establish safety and pollution standards to be observed in the interests of the communities in which companies operate. But companies may acknowledge obligations not set out in law: they may, for example, feel and act on an obligation to improve the quality of life in the community in which they operate by sponsoring community activities.

A good example of this approach to community relations is

found in the experience of company towns in remote areas of northern Canada. These towns are dominated by one industry and usually by one company. In Fort McMurray in northern Alberta the company which moved in to exploit the oil sands just north of the town became the town's principal employer in a very short space of time and, as a major source of employment in the area, drew large numbers of people into the town. It quickly became involved in local problems, caused by the rapid influx of people: it set up a subsidiary company to build houses for newcomers to the town, and sponsored education and recreation programmes to meet the needs of the town's growing population. The company also developed training programmes for the region's native people, to enable them to take advantage of employment opportunities on the company's sites.

Obligations to the community are defined partly by necessity and partly through choice. In the case we've just looked at, the company was the cause of many of the problems experienced by the community – rapid increase in population, shortages of housing and strain on social services – and was bound to become involved in solving these problems.

Another example of a community relations programme developed out of necessity is provided by British Nuclear Fuels Limited (BNFL) recent efforts to re-establish its credibility with local and national communities.

The company's Sellafield nuclear plant in Cumbria, in the north of England, provides direct employment for 13,000 people, but a number of incidents there over recent years have called its safety into question and led to calls for its closure.

BNFL has responded to criticisms of safety and local community fears that the plant is dangerous by opening the facility to the public. Changing public perceptions of the plant has involved building a new visitors' centre on the site and working with national and local tourist boards, as well as local schools, to attract visitors. In addition to these efforts aimed at bringing people on to the Sellafield site, the company has supported local community projects. The steps taken have produced results, bringing about positive changes in the way Sellafield is perceived. These changes have been measured through public opinion research, but are also indicated in the numbers of people passing through the Sellafield Visitors' Centre. In 1986–87, the centre was said by the English Tourist Board to be the country's fastest growing tourist attraction.[1]

Sellafield provides an example of a compay's use of community relations to re-win public support essential to the continuing operation of the facility and of the nuclear industry. Public hostility and fear led the company to change its approach to community relations.

Companies and other organizations will involve themselves in community relations activities for reasons other than necessity. They may subscribe to a set of values which motivate them to put something back into the communities of which they are part, or make a commitment to support specific activities, such as medical research or the arts. The Digital Equipment Company in the United Kingdom is a major sponsor of dance in the country, Royal Insurance has become a benefactor of the Royal Shakespeare Company and a group of companies including IBM and BP support Business in the Arts, an initiative aimed at providing training opportunities and other assistance to arts organizations to improve their own management practices.

Community relations practice raises questions regarding corporate social responsibility. What is corporate social responsibility? Does the business organization have social responsibilities that go beyond responsibilities to shareholders and responsibilities to manage its affairs as efficiently as possible?

Decisions on community relations activities

There is no simple guide to decision-making on community relations activities. If community relations activities are seen as a means to an end, then they can be used to help in the achievement of specific objectives – for example, to counter criticisms of plans to expand a factory in a small town. If they are seen as part of the organization's social obligations, then decision-making is harder and involves some of these considerations:

- What are the organization's obligations to the community of which it is part? One answer, put forward by the Nobel prize-winning economist, Milton Friedman, is that as far as business organizations are concerned their only responsibility is to make a profit, within the bounds of legality and ethical custom. He suggested in 1970 that: 'there is one and only one social responsibility of business – to use its resources and engage in activities designed to increase its profits.'[2] Another view is that, since business draws from the community the resources it needs to generate wealth and produce profit for its shareholders, it should return benefits to the community over and above the goods and services that it provides. In practice, the answer will be provided by the organization itself: what obligations is it prepared to acknowledge?
- What are the organization's own objectives in relation to the community? What sort of support does the organization need from the community: What can be done to counter opposition from the community to the organization's intentions or activities?
- What might the community need or expect from the organization and how far can the organization go towards meeting community expectations?
- Can the organization's interests and objectives be reconciled with community needs and expectations to mutual benefit?
- If the organization acknowledges obligations to the community, and seeks to reconcile its own objectives with community needs and interests, which community relations approaches will be most effective?

Community relations activities are driven by mixed motives – self-interest (more or less enlightened) and genuine desire to make a contribution to the community. A study published in 1987 by The Conference Board in the United States found that a number of factors influence a company's involvement in the community. It concluded that many companies focus on community issues that make it possible for them to combine business opportunities with community improvement. In the United States this approach has led many companies to move away from corporate support of the arts to focus on community concerns for the state of the country's educational system. Education is described in an article by Mary Lowengard in the Public Relations Society of America's Journal for October 1989,[3] as a community issue, a corporate bottom-line issue and a national survival issue.

In considering community relations activities, it is important for organizations to be clear about the objectives they are pursuing so that they can see how possible community relations activities might help towards the realization of those objectives. Clarity regarding objectives will make it easier to weigh up possible community relations options: for example, response to requests for sponsorship.

Decisions regarding community relations activities should also be based on an assessment of community needs. It might be advantageous for a company based in a small town to put funding into a community arts festival as a means of achieving short-term visibility in the community, but the community might have greater need for longer-term investment in an urban regeneration project. The company would then be faced with the task of balancing its own interests in gaining short-term recognition with the community's long-term needs.

Prominent companies receive many requests for assistance and sponsorship from organizations in the community and need to have in place some means of choosing between these requests. Information regarding company priorities and resources is important in this process, as is knowledge of community needs. Companies need also to decide how far they are prepared to meet community expectations. In the United Kingdom, about 275 companies – including major companies such as Glaxo and the National Westminster Bank – have joined The Per Cent Club, committing half a per cent or more of their pre-tax (UK) profits to support of community initiatives. Such a step sets limits on the amount of assistance to be made available and decisions can be made with knowledge of limits imposed.

The task of any individual or group having to decide upon community relations activities is to assess:

- The organization's objectives
- Community needs and requests for assistance
- Available resources, approaches and techniques

Approaches to community relations

Approaches to community relations include making contributions to community organizations and active involvement in community projects, issues or events.

Contributions may be made directly to charitable organizations, arts organizations, or institutions involved in education and research. Contributions will be made within the limits of the organization's willingness to provide direct financial support and decided upon by named individuals within the organization through some approval process, formal or informal. Responsibility for making decisions or recommendations regarding contributions will often fall, at first, to personnel or public relations departments but contributions are more often decided upon finally at the most senior levels of major organizations.

Community relations practitioners in the United States have observed that companies are now less willing to give contributions without some direct involvement in how contributions are used. This trend, which is also apparent in the United Kingdom, makes the task of deciding upon contributions, their level and destination more difficult because organizations deciding upon contributions have to be sure that the beneficiaries of contributions have goals, objectives and activities that are compatible with those of donor organizations.

The benefits to donor organizations of making contributions are long-term and indirect ones which contribute to the building of reputation over time. For example, Royal Insurance's substantial support of the Royal Shakespeare Company brings some immediate benefit, but greater long-term benefit. In the short term, Royal Insurance is recognized for making a major contribution at a time when the theatre company's financial position is not strong, but in the longer term its reputation as a patron of the arts will be enhanced. It will also have the benefits of association with the programmes of the Royal Shakespeare Company.

Sponsorship involves more immediate benefit to sponsoring companies. It associates the name of a company directly with a highly visible public activity, chosen because it enables the company's name to be placed before groups of people particularly important to it. Large sponsorships are given to support televised sporting events which attract national and international followings, for example golf tournaments or football competitions. Dunhill Holdings, a company which includes a number of component companies marketing luxury goods world-wide, sponsors the Dunhill Cup, a major golf tournament which generates television and other media coverage world-wide and is of direct interest to Dunhill's potential customers.

Decisions on sponsorship need to take into account the benefits that can be foreseen from participation in the activities which are to be sponsored. For example, the manufacturer of outdoor equipment is likely to be interested in sponsoring a high-profile expedition if its own products are going to be used. Sponsorship is a growing area of public relations practice and a large number of consultancies specialise in sponsorship work, matching client ambitions to sponsor visible public events and activities with opportunities available and helping groups looking for sponsorship to find suitable sponsors. A full list of consultancies specializing in sponsorship is set out in directories such as the Hollis directory mentioned in

Chapter 4 (on page 64).

Now, community relations activities tend to involve companies and other organizations directly in community projects and issues. In the United Kingdom, organizations such as Business in the Community exist to enable business organizations to become actively involved in community projects, such as those directed towards inner city regeneration. Large companies may be drawn directly in to work on the solution of social problems by central government or by organizations such as the Confederation of British Industry. Active involvement of companies in the solution of social problems includes:

■ Secondment, where company executives are seconded for a period of time to work as a members of community organizations to provide their expertise to the management of community projects
■ Short-term participation of business leaders in community projects to, for example, co-operate with local and central government to work for urban regeneration and economic development

Direct involvement by company executives in community concerns opens up possibilities for them to help shape public debate, or to intervene in public debate to mediate between groups with possibly conflicting interests. Whether or not business executives want to go this far is one of the open questions of community relations practice, but in the United States these possibilities are seen as providing companies with an opportunity to become true partners in the community.

Managing community relations

As another specialist area within public relations, community relations can be managed within a public relations department as one of a number of tasks carried by a senior public relations manager. In a larger public relations department, a section of the department may be devoted to community relations, overseeing charitable donations, contributions, sponsorship and community project work. Where the organization is unable or unwilling to sustain public relations staff, some allocation of senior management time will need to be made to community relations work, or some other arrangements will have to be made to make decisions on requests from the community for contributions or sponsorships.

A study of community relations practice in the United States found that community relations responsibilities are carried by specialist staff alongside other responsibilities. It is, for most of the people involved in the practice, a part-time occupation. Community relations responsibilities are often decentralized, allocated to line managers in branch offices, plants and service outlets. There are strong arguments for this approach, where a company is itself decentralized, because it allows local managers to be responsive to local community needs. Central community relations staff can act as a resource to line managers, providing advice on approaches to community relations and training in community relations techniques.

In other arrangements personnel departments or senior managers make decisions on requests for support from community organizations or charities.

From a management perspective, it is important to know where the organization's interests lie, and how they can be met with available staff resources. The smallest organization will still have relationships with the community in which it operates to consider. For the larger organization, with more resources, community relations will require that the organization under-stands its own objectives and where community relations activities can contribute to the achievement of identified objectives. It can then make decisions regarding the allocation of staff time and resources to community relations activities. It can also make use of the most appropriate community relations techniques.

Community relations techniques

A number of community relations techniques are available to the community relations practitioner, or to the manager who has to take on community relations responsibilities:

- The organization has resources at its disposal which it can make available to the community: these resources may be financial, material or human. Financial resources may provide funding for community projects, or allow community groups to pursue their activities. Material resources may include vehicles, or goods needed by community groups. Human resources will include the executives of the organization, who may be able to provide managerial expertise to community groups. It is important that the organization has in place a policy which makes clear how its resources may be made available to the community and a means of making decisions about requests for assistance, or about initiatives that will involve the organization in community relations activities
- The organization can apply its resources in a number of ways:
  - in response to requests for assistance or funding from community organizations
  - as a result of careful examination of organization objectives to see which community activities should be supported
  - as a result of research which indicates which community needs should be addressed by the organization
- Communication techniques used in community relations can include some of the techniques we have already seen in use – for example in looking at British Nuclear Fuels' work with its Sellafield site, we saw how the company made use of an 'open house' technique to allow members of the community to visit the plant site. Opening facilities to the community is one way of allowing the community into the organization to see what the organization's work involves.

Other communication techniques used include public meetings and exhibitions. Public meetings are often used when an organization wishes to get public reaction to its plans. Exhibitions, in local town halls, libraries or meeting places, can be an effective means of presenting the organization's plans to the public and inviting comment

■ The community relations practitioner is essentially a link or a means of liaison between the organization and the community. Just as the practitioner of media relations aims to put journalists in contact with sources of information, so the community member wants to be able to communicate with the people in the organization who can answer his or her concerns. It is the community relations practitioner's task to make sure that this communication occurs

Some of these techniques can be seen in a 1988 community relations project devised by British Telecom and Essex Police, in the United Kingdom's East Anglia region.[4] Both organizations wanted to achieve certain objectives: the police wanted to establish better relationships with young people generally, while British Telecom wanted to reduce vandalism of its property and demonstrate involvement with the community.

The two organizations chose the vehicle of a community relations programme to help to improve the quality of life in the region. The programme involved a social and environmental campaign which encouraged groups of young people to select a square mile and devise ways in which they could improve the area, environmentally and socially. The campaign was run over a short period, which included the school summer holidays, allowing sufficient time to complete constructive projects.

The collaboration between the two organizations involved Essex Police in providing manpower and promotional help and British Telecom in organizing and funding the project.

The campaign was launched with the assistance of youth leaders, local councils, environmental groups, education

authorities and teachers to encourage young people to partici-
pate and attracted considerable publicity at the outset. Media
interest in the campaign was sustained throughout the project
and a number of teams of young people who took part were
interviewed for radio, television and newspaper features.

Over 350 teams of young people took part in the campaign,
which had been explained by its organizers to 24 school
assemblies throughout the region. Seven teams were chosen to
make final presentations of their ideas to a panel of judges,
who assessed the research, initiative and enterprise which had
gone into the presentations. The winning group was chosen a
week later at British Telecom's regional headquarters.

The project, in addition to providing a worthwhile experience for 2,000 young people in the region, allowed police
liaison officers to talk to over 8,000 children. A number of
environmental schemes were proposed and completed.

Systems Publicity, the regional community relations consultants who worked on the project with British Telecom and
Essex Police, and who were a main contact point for information about the project, felt that the Square Mile Project had
helped young people in the region to think seriously about
environmental issues. At the same time, it allowed the regional
police force to make contract with young people and involved
British Telecom in the community in a way which enabled it
to address some of its concerns about vandalism.

This case illustrates a number of other features of community relations activities. They can involve imaginative collaboration between organizations with complementary interests and
benefit all participants. In this case the two sponsoring
organizations achieved their objectives, young people in the
region were able to take part in an interesting and worthwhile
project, and other members of the community were also able
to benefit. For example, one project involved the building of
a pond and rockery in the garden of an old people's home.

The two organizations and their advisers made extensive use
of communication techniques to stimulate interest in the
project and to encourage young people to become involved.

They also enlisted the support of community organizations, schools and local government, as well as a television celebrity, to ensure interest in the project. The media were involved from the outset, and were provided with information from the project at its launch and as project teams began their work. Communicating the project's scope to groups of young people brought the police into face-to-face contact with school groups and also kept them in contact as they provided packs of information about the project to potential entrants.

Summary points

Community relations is another specialized area of public relations practice which takes in relations with the community – local, regional, national and international. Community relations practice quickly raises questions about the social responsibilities of organizations and about their obligations to the communities of which they are part. Community relations can be approached as a means to an end, another way of helping organizations to achieve their objectives. But organizations approach community relations with mixed objectives, only some of which bear directly on the organizations' own self-interests. The difficulty in making decisions regarding community relations is found in trying to reconcile organization interests with community interests. Ultimately, what is good for the community should also be good for the organization which operates within it.

There are a number of approaches to community relations involving donations or contributions to community organizations, sponsorship of community activities, or direct involvement in community projects, issues or concerns. As in other areas of public relations practice, communication is used to establish the links between organization and community groups and between community groups that will be necessary for the success of community relations projects.

Management options for community relations activities include allocating tasks involved to specialist staff, within or outside the organization, or devolving responsibility for community relations activities to line managers or other staff. What is important in considering community relations activities is that organizations need to be clear about their own objectives in relation to the community and to be able to see how community relations activities will help them to achieve those objectives.

CHAPTER SIX

INVESTOR RELATIONS

INVESTOR RELATIONS IS a specialist's practice, requiring detailed knowledge of financial markets and legal requirements for public disclosure of financial information by companies, as well as a well-developed understanding of investor psychology and the means of communicating with investors and their advisors. The practice developed extensively in the United States[1] in the 1950s and now needs to take into account the complexity of the global capital market, corporate takeover activity across national borders, increasingly sophisticated investors and international developments which can affect investor confidence around the world in a matter of moments. As this is written, continuing tension in the Middle East is having an effect on investor confidence, with stock markets in the world's major financial centres fluctuating daily on rumours of war and hopes for peace.

Investor relations has emerged as a significant practice in the United Kingdom over the past ten years, as a consequence of changes in the City of London, deregulation of the stock market, the encouragement by government of wider share-ownership and a number of highly-publicized flotations, privatizations and takeover battles – what one commentator called the 'mega-bid boom' of the mid 1980s.

In this chapter, we will look at management questions raised by the practice of investor relations, and briefly at some of the techniques of investor relations. These are also dealt with in a book by Neil Ryder and Michael Regester,[2] one of the first books to be written which takes a United Kingdom rather than a United States view of the practice. Their view is that investor relations is the financial end of the communication function rather than the communications end of the financial function.

As in other areas of public relations practice, there are differing views about where investor relations fits into the overall management task. Is the practice one that should fit within the responsibilities of a company's finance director, or should it be the responsibility of a specialist, working under the supervision of a senior manager responsible for public relations activities?

Tom Burke, writing in the International Public Relations Review,[3] suggests that some aspects of the investor relations role, such as the tasks involved in communicating with shareholders through reports, videos and media releases, can be dealt with by the competent public relations practitioner. The successful investor relations specialist also needs what Burke calls 'Wall Street seasoning' – knowledge of financial markets, financial statements, investment analyst information requirements and specific strategies for communicating with select audiences. He also points out that special skills are needed by the investor relations adviser who should be able to contribute at times of contest for corporate control, in the takeover battle.

Investor relations and public relations

As we saw in Chapter 1 the overall aim of public relations practice is to have an effect on the behaviour of groups of people, so that they will behave in ways favourable to the organization or individual on whose behalf public relations is being practised. Financial public relations concentrates on those groups of people whose financial support is needed by the organization. These will include present and potential shareholders and the investment community. The behaviour sought from these groups will be shown in decisions to maintain, initiate or support investment in the organization.

Financial public relations activities are directed towards

finding the financial support that the organization will need to pursue its objectives, through a complex of relationships. Investor relations practice is concerned with investors in particular, and with investor perceptions of the value of shares, the make-up of investor support, lines of communication to investors, and the advice and information provided to investors by the organization itself, by investment analysts and by the financial press.

Perceptions of share value

The aim in investor relations activities is to ensure that investors develop an accurate picture of the value of the shares in which they are being asked to invest, or to sustain an investment. As Neil Ryder and Michael Regester emphasize, there is potential for long-term damage to a company if expectations regarding the value of a particular company's shares are too high.

Perceptions of share value are built by communication of the company's strengths and weaknesses, past and present performance and future prospects, realistically assessed. Investor relations programmes are intended to meet needs for information about a company from both investors, present and potential, and those who can influence their decisions.

The task facing investor relations practitioners is to collaborate with senior management to develop objectives for relationships with actual and potential shareholders, and then to refine and agree information that will make up communication with investor groups. The results of this collaboration are apparent in the work that has been done recently in the United Kingdom on flotations and privatizations. As a result of government policy, a number of organizations which were previously under state ownership and run as public sector organizations have been, and are still being, returned to private sector ownership. Examples include: British Airways, British Gas and British Telecom. Each privatization has been accompanied by carefully crafted programmes aimed at ensuring maximum interest on the part of potential investors. These programmes have been very effective. British Airways, for example, was the subject of 1.1 million applications for shares in the company when it was privatized.

Flotations have also generated wide public interest in share ownership. When, in 1986, the TSB Group, made up of Trustee Savings Banks, changed its status and offered shares to the public in a well-orchestrated flotation, there were five million applications.[4] The flotation had a number of phases. First, in mid-1985, a corporate advertising campaign to build awareness of the TSB's services and strengths was initiated. This was followed by advertising to support the flotation itself. The actual flotation was delayed by legal questions concerning the effects of the Group's change of status on the rights of depositors, but it was relaunched once these questions had been resolved in June, 1986.

The flotation communications programme was managed by the Group's communications staff, and regular tracking studies of the attitudes of potential investors were carried out, monthly at first, then weekly, in the final phases of the campaign. From July, 1986, the flotation campaign used advertising, press conferences, direct mail techniques, posters, road shows and audio-visual presentations. Later in the campaign, the prospectus giving full details of the share offer was published in national newspapers, with application forms. Seven million prospectuses were produced.

The tracking studies demonstrated the success of the flotation campaign. At its outset, 29 per cent of the public knew about the offer, and 22 per cent expressed interest in buying shares. Just before the offer for sale closed, 81 per cent were aware of the share flotation, and 29 per cent said they were interested in buying shares. The Group's research suggested that 2.5 million applications for shares would be rceived, but this number was doubled by publicity given to the share offering during the actual offer period of 12 days.

Campaigns developed to support privatizations and flotations also illustrate the benefits of careful planning, skilful use of research and disposition of resources. At times of defence against a hostile takeover bid investor relations are marked by hasty decision-making, considerable pressures on decision-makers and the rapid assembly of groups of advisers. The hostile takeover bid may constitute a crisis for the organization which is the subject of the bid, and may call into question the crisis management abilities of its senior management group and advisers. We will be looking at crisis management in more detail in Chapter 8, but insight into what happens at the time of a hostile takeover bid is provided by the attempted takeover in 1985 of Allied-Lyons, a UK brewing and foods group, by Elders IXL, an Australian conglomerate with strong interests in brewing.

Allied-Lyons' resistance to the bid was followed by a Financial Times journalist, Christopher Parkes,[5] who was able to sit in on meetings of senior management and its advisers to record events. His summary of the defence also shows quite clearly the organizational arrangements that have to be made to communicate with shareholders.

The company's response to the bid was managed by a 'war cabinet', which met weekly and was advised by a team from the company's merchant bankers, S.G. Warburg. The war cabinet was also advised by a shareholders' policy committee, charged with maintaining links with investment institutions and brokers, and a communications council, made up of members of the war cabinet as well as representatives from the company's public relations consultancy and advertising agency. The shareholders' policy committee and the communications council met weekly, but another committee which drew together company staff and advisers and was headed by the company's group investment controller, Tony Pratt, met more frequently. The communications council and the Pratt committee were responsible for contacts with the media, politicians, internal management groups, tenants of the company's licensed premises, unions, and other internal and external contacts.

Reflecting on the defence later, the company's chairman pointed out that it took time to get the company's defence committees together, and that at first the company was reacting to events on a day-to-day basis. The defence, which the Financial Times followed for over fifty days into its aftermath, was finally successful and the Elders conglomerate moved on to another target. This, however, was not before the company discovered how ill-prepared it was to defend itself. Internal communications were poor, and the company was not able to present arguments against the bid effectively to its own staff at the outset. This changed as the defence progressed and members of the senior management met with 650 managers from all parts of the company to explain the company's position.

Efforts put into external communications, through advertising and through direct personal contact between the company's senior management and institutional investors, eventually convinced the latter of the strength of the Allied defence. In the early days of the defence, the company had access to the results of surveys of shareholders' and tenants' opinions, which showed how the company's position was viewed, and how the bidding company's intentions were seen.

The account of the defence shows how much of the discussion of approaches to defending the company was focused on relationships between the company and groups important to it, such as employees, individual and institutional investors, and on communication.

Planning for defence against takeover

A takeover attempt may represent a crisis for a company. As we will see in Chapter 8, a crisis is an unexpected event which threatens an organization's interests and possibly even its existence. Public relations staff with specific responsibilities for investor relations can prepare for possible takeover bids by:

■ Developing a crisis management plan which takes the possibility of a takeover into account, and outlines a response

- Ensuring that accurate information is being provided to important groups so that company share price is as strong as can be justified
- Identifying present owners of company shares through examination of the company's share register, and tracking changes in ownership
- Developing material for use in communication with key groups at the time of any bid, and deciding who will speak for the company to the media, company employees, analysts, suppliers and customers
- Developing senior management knowledge of the plans that have been made

In one company that I had the opportunity to observe before and following a hostile takeover bid, the company's advisers were unable to convince senior managers of the need to prepare against the bid before it came, even though strong rumours that a bid was to be made were picked up some months earlier.

Managing investor relations

Building relationships with potential or current investors depends on adequate knowledge of their interests and motivations. This means that the management of investor relations activities must be based on research, which will provide a profile of actual or potential investor groups, as well as of groups which influence investors' decisions, such as investment analysts or financial journalists.

Communication with actual or potential investors can take a number of forms, including required communication such as annual reports and communication through other media, for example the financial press. The company that wishes its position to be fully understood and for its shareholders to become familiar with its strategy and operations will take care to communicate with them rather more than is required under strict legal rules. Communication is a means of influencing shareholders' decisions regarding their investments. It is also a means of generating goodwill which can be drawn upon at time of need, although the Elders bid for Allied-Lyons led one Allied employee to say '. . . in the end it's all a matter of price. Loyalty goes out of the window if the price is right.'

The tasks to be carried out to manage the company's investor relations will be determined by:

- The company's position
- Its need for shareholder support
- The number and type of shareholders who have invested in the company
- The vulnerability of the company to a possible takeover
- The company's ambitions regarding acquisitions

The tasks involved will need to be overseen by the organization's senior management group, with the most senior manager having final responsibility for investor relations. This responsibility can be delegated to a member of the senior management team, and can be properly discharged only through co-operation on the part of finance, legal, marketing and communication staff.

I recently advised a company listed on one of the United Kingdom's markets. It had no public relations department, but was advised on investor relations matters by a consultancy which specialized in financial public relations. The consultancy reported to the finance director, while another member of the company's senior management group was responsible for the company's marketing activities. Legal matters and some of the company's internal communications were managed by other senior managers. Since the company was planning to expand, its various communications activities, including investor relations, were brought under the closer supervision of one senior manager.

The ideal qualifications for a senior manager overseeing investor relations are, according to Michael Regester and Neil Ryder, insight into the company's operations, derived from access to the company's senior management group, and good knowledge of finance and of the sector in which the company is operating. Good communications skills are essential, and messages developed as part of the company's investor relations programmes must be consistent with other messages developed by the company for other audiences. This requires the investor relations manager to be aware of the content of other communications programmes.

Another example of how a number of communications activities, including investor relations, are co-ordinated is provided by the British company NFC plc. The company was the subject of a buy-out in 1982 when members of the company, until then owned by the British government, staged the largest employee buy-out ever completed in the United Kingdom. By 1988, employee shareholding in the company amounted to nearly 82 per cent of issued capital. The company has the task of keeping its shareholders, who are also its employees, well informed regarding its progress. Internal communications with employees, and investor relations are major tasks for the company's communications department, which also draws on consultancy advice in its approach to the investment community.

In investor relations, communication programmes are directed at investors themselves, but also at groups who can influence them, such as investment analysts and the financial press. Both groups provide channels of communication between companies and shareholders. An article on the role of City (financial) editors on Britain's national newspapers in *Business*[6] magazine explores the relationships between journalists and company public relations staff who provide them with information, and suggests that favourable press comment becomes especially important when a company is involved in a takeover battle. It is a prize to be won by public relations practitioners whose efforts lead to some resentment on the part of journalists who feel manipulated by public relations staff. Despite this, the exchange of information between analysts, public relations staff and journalists does allow for material to appear in analysts' newsletters, on the financial pages of newspapers and in radio and television programmes, all of which serve to inform investors.

Techniques of investor relations

Of all the communication techniques available in investor relations, the annual report is considered by many practitioners to be the most important corporate communication document produced by an organization. Senior management must be involved in its preparation from the outset, so that the report can express a clear statement of the company's strategy and direction to important audiences.

Choice of techniques to be used in investor relations will be determined partly through research into the information needs of important groups. For example, the campaign developed by Dewe Rogerson to support the privatization of the water authorities in England and Wales in 1989 drew on a research data base which defined the interests of private investors. The campaign had a number of audiences: investors, influencers such as the media and brokers' analysts, advisers and pressure groups who were opposed to the privatization.[7]

The water privatization was a complex one made up of the simultaneous flotation of ten separate companies, and the communications programmes which supported it included:

- Design (the development of an identity for the overall programme)
- Brochures and information sheets
- The establishment of a share information office to receive enquiries and send information and prospectuses to over four million people
- Direct mail, which was used to send information to 20 million people
- Roadshow presentations, which made use of video
- National and regional media relations
- Employee communication

■ Advertising

Research was used to establish investors' interests, to develop campaign concepts and to track the impact of the campaign. The campaign led to 2.7 million applications for shares, and to over-subscription to the share offer. This was at a time when campaign planners could foreseee a number of obstacles to the success of the share offer, such as the opposition of environmental groups to the water industry.

More modest programmes of investor relations activity will still draw on many of the same techniques. Information that companies are required to make available to shareholders and potential investors should be presented in the most attractive way possible, to give a feeling for the companies involved. Companies are advised to go beyond bare legal obligations to ensure that they provide a full and accurate picture of their operations.

The future of investor relations

Evidence from the United States suggests that the investor relations role will increase in importance, for a number of reasons. All issues that affect the company's cost of capital are coming into the domain of the investor relations practitioner who is also, in the United States, called upon to help translate the technical language describing the company's financial position for shareholders' benefit. In Europe, the creation of the Single Market, which will include an internal market in financial services, will influence the practice of investor relations. Practitioners in the United States and Europe will have to be global in outlook, and able to understand the application of national and international regulations to investor relations practice.

Some doubts are emerging in the United States about whether or not investor relations practitioners are equal to the tasks they now face. This concern is based on practitioners' lack of qualification for the detailed work that investor relations practice requires. We'll return in Chapter 11 to questions regarding the qualifications of public relations staff.

Developments in the United Kingdom, as the European market organizes to compete on a world level, will follow changes in legislation and regulations governing financial institutions and practices at the European as well as national levels. These changes will bear on the practice of investor relations and the qualifications of investor relations practitioners.

Investor relations – summary points

Investor relations is a specialized practice, requiring well-developed public relations and communications skills and a full knowledge of financial markets and the way companies work as financial entities. The manager in a company with investor relations needs will have to decide on approaches to managing the tasks involved. With adequate resources, responsibilities for investor relations may be given to a senior manager who has access to the senior management group. Co-ordination with other public relations activities is essential, so that activities are mutually reinforcing and consistent.

Research to develop an understanding of the company's shareholder support (actual and potential) should underlie all investor relations activities, which will involve use of a range of communication techniques. Some of these techniques will be limited by legal requirements governing the disclosure of information. As a general rule, companies should be prepared to go beyond the barest legal requirements to ensure that investors have full information as a basis for their investment decisions.

Managers may have to face the decision of whether or not to draw on outside advisers on investor relations matters. Outside advisers may be vital in a defence against unwanted takeover. Investor relations now requires a global outlook on the part of practitioners, as well as detailed knowledge of the regulations and practices current in world markets. Managers who have to draw on advice in investor relations matters will have trouble finding practitioners who are sufficiently qualified to help them. This is not a criticism of investor relations practitioners but a recognition of the difficulty they have in keeping up with complex developments in a number of markets around the world.

CHAPTER SEVEN

MARKETING AND PUBLIC RELATIONS

A COMMONLY-HELD VIEW is that public relations is, or should be, part of marketing and managed as a marketing activity. The British publication *PR Week*, a weekly which reports on the public relations industry, regularly describes it as a marketing service activity, and significant numbers of its practitioners ally their activities directly with marketing activities. In the United States, the link between public relations and marketing has been debated at national conferences of the Public Relations Society of America, and the conclusion was reached at one such conference that marketing is public relations' link to the bottom line – public relations makes its contribution to organizational effectiveness and profitability through marketing.

In marketing practice, marketers attend to and manipulate four key variables as they manage their activities: the products they are concerned with, product price, promotion and the place where products are to be offered for sale. Concern for these four variables involves marketers in product development, pricing decisions, marketing communications, logistics and distribution, and the work and training of sales staff. Some commentators in recent years have seen marketing as the central management task, concerned with creating, satisfying and keeping customers, making sure that products are available to customers and that they are products that customers will want to buy.

From a marketing perspective, public relations is part of promotional activities and an aid to customer relations. When the marketer considers options for marketing communications, public relations is bracketed with advertising and other forms of promotional communications, for example at point of sale. Writers on marketing, such as Philip Kotler,[1] one of the leading US commentators on marketing practice, have supported this view and suggested that public relations should be managed as part of marketing.

Kotler has gone on to broaden the concept of marketing. Marketing becomes megamarketing, which he describes as the application of economic, psychological, political and PR skills to gain the co-operation of a number of parties in order to enter and or to operate successfully in a given market.

Marketing and public relations activities can be managed together, for example in a marketing department, where personnel concerned with advertising and public relations report to a marketing manager. Public relations activities are managed as part of overall marketing activities.

Occasionally, marketing activities may be managed in a public relations department, for example in a university setting, where community relations and fund-raising activities may also form part of the responsibility of a director of external relations. Marketing activities do not make up the sum of such departments' work, but are managed to support the presentation of programmes and services to clients such as potential students.

Two other models can be followed in the management of marketing and public relations activities. Both see marketing and public relations activities allocated to different staff members or staff groups. In the first, marketing and public relations staff work separately, but are required to work together where their concerns overlap, for example on product promotion. The second approach also involves two separate departments with the slight difference that there are no obvious areas of overlap and the relationship between the two departments has to be negotiated on a project-by-project basis. There is obvious scope for conflict in this arrangement but it is one which can also be of benefit to the organization sustaining it. Benefit is derived as both departments are able to contribute their perspectives to the discussion of management courses of action.

Public relations is a practice which complements marketing activities, but one that should not be absorbed into them, for some reasons which we should now explore.

Marketing has enjoyed a special place in management for a number of years now, because in a highly competitive world the techniques which identify market opportunities, contribute to the development and sale of suitable products, and help to maintain and build customer satisfaction and market share are so obviously valuable. At the same time, however, the full task of management cannot be reduced to marketing, any more than the full task of management can be limited to concern for the organization's human resources, or to the organization's need for financial and material resources. Management involves bringing together perspectives on tasks to be carried out, decision-making and action on information received, and checks on performance. In this, marketing provides important perspectives and information, as well as techniques which are of proven value in helping to realize managerial objectives.

The marketing approach has limitations. Its critics ask why, if marketing is supposed to increase an organization's sensitivity to the market-place, and to consumer needs and expectations, the years of marketing prominence have also seen a growth in consumerism – consumer protest against inferior products and questionable marketing practices, and the banding together of consumers in organizations such as the UK's Consumers' Association to protect their interests.

Marketing is based on beliefs in growth, production, the encouragement of consumption, and the persuasion of large numbers of people to buy, to consume, to acquire and to discard. These beliefs do not sit easily alongside doubts which have now surfaced in public debate about 'green' issues and environmental conservation as to the wisdom of current levels of consumption. Business organizations, grouped in associations such as the International Chamber of Commerce, are

now beginning to support the idea of 'sustainable development', development and growth within limits. Limits on
growth have been talked about for a number of years, but as
we get closer now to having to act within limits, our thinking
regarding approaches to management, marketing among
them, will have to change.

This is where public relations still has its full contribution to
make. Public relations is a complement and a corrective to the
marketing approach. As a complement, it provides information and techniques which support marketing efforts. The
techniques of communication used in public relations are
available to marketing, and can be used in support of product
and sales promotion. These techniques of communication fall
under the description of marketing communication when used
in marketing.

By building important relations and contributing to the
central relationship with customers, public relations can help
to develop a social environment in which marketing activities
will be more likely to be effective. For example, in the
Prudential case (see Chapter 3 pages 40–42), corporate public
relations activities aimed at establishing the Prudential's new
corporate identity and at informing important groups such as
financial journalists, investment analysts, and the company's
own staff that the company had changed in response to the
changing competitive environment all contributed to creating
an environment in which it would be easier to market the
company's financial, real estate or insurance services. The
corporate identity programme was developed in 1986 to help
the company take advantage of prevailing market conditions.
These have now changed, but the thrust of the company's
corporate public relations activities at the time was complementary to the company's marketing objectives.

However, public relations is also a corrective to the marketing approach, because the perspective on which the practice is
based is broader than the marketing perspective. Public
relations can raise questions which the marketing approach,
with its focus on the market, products, distribution channels

and customers, and its orientation towards growth and consumption, cannot. Public relations concerns are with the
relations of groups one to another, and with the interplay of
conflicting and competing interests in social relationships. In
an excellent case study which showed how a Dutch coffee
company was forced by community protest to drop its use of
coffee imported from Angola, then a Portuguese colony, Geert
Hofstede, a writer on international management practice,
demonstrated the value of the public relations perspective.[2]
From the public relations perspective, it is possible to challenge
the predominating values within an organization – not for the
sake of challenge, but because an organization which has failed
to appreciate that the values and interests prevailing in the
outside society have changed may be in danger. The marketing
perspective, despite suggestions that marketers can make use
of research to remain sensitive to the outside world, cannot
mount the same constructive challenge, because of the values
and beliefs on which the marketing approach is based.

Public relations' perspective, capacity for challenge and
potential contribution to management decision-making are
diminished if not removed by bringing public relations in
under marketing, or by seeing public relations as a marketing
service activity.

In practice, senior managers will need to be satisfied that the
benefits of the public relations perspective are available to the
organization. If a decision is made to staff a marketing
department and to include within it a public relations staff
member or section, then the managers making such a decision
need to be sure that the public relations perspective can be
fully expressed under this arrangement.

Questions to be asked by senior managers thinking about the
relationship between marketing and public relations and
considering how to incorporate both functions into the
organization are:

- Are the organization's objectives mainly marketing
  objectives?

- What are the organization's resources? Can the organization afford to staff both functions? If not, what sort of
  individual might be able to carry both functions, or should
  one be carried by senior management?
- What organizational arrangements should be made to
  incorporate both functions? Options are:
  - retention of both by senior management
  - retention of one by senior management, with a specialist
    staff member or staff group responsible for the other
  - a specialist staff member or group having responsibility
    for both functions, for example, a marketing services
    department with a public relations section, or an external
    affairs department with a marketing services section
  - two specialist staff members or departments working
    independently, but with overlapping responsibilities
  - two specialist staff members or departments working
    independently, collaborating as required on a project-by-
    project basis
  - the use of outside staff to carry out either or both of the
    functions, working directly with senior management or
    with internal staff

Public relations as a complement to marketing activities

For organizations mainly concerned with marketing goods and
services, all other activities will contribute to this central task.
Staff will be chosen for their marketing skills, resources
available will be allocated to allow for maximum support of
marketing activities, the organizations will be structured so as
to be as responsive to their customers, and so on. Public
relations will be a complement and support to marketing
activities.

A good example is provided by Dunhill Holdings,[3] a British-
based holding company which has assembled a portfolio of
luxury goods products, growing the portfolio skilfully around
the Dunhill brand name. Its products include menswear,
leather, jewellery, fragrance, and fountain pens. The

company's board decided early in the 1980s that its greatest asset was the Dunhill name, and the name was carefully used in the holding company's business of international brand name marketing. Dunhill products are available and advertised world-wide.

A number of techniques are used to sustain and develop the company's brand-names. The company makes extensive use of advertising, to build brand awareness, to communicate the range and desirability of the company's products and to position the Dunhill brand as one offering outstanding quality, craftsmanship and style. Advertising is placed in publications such as major inflight magazines and key tourist media.

In addition to advertising, the company is involved in a number of sponsorships, which bring the company's name in front of millions of television viewers around the world, in the case of the Dunhill Cup, an annual golf tournament which attracts the world's finest golfers and is watched on prime-time television. Extensive coverage is also given to the event in the world's quality media. The company also sponsors the Queen's Cup Polo Competition, one of the most prestigious events in the international polo calendar.

Public relations activities are managed as part of the company's overall marketing efforts, complementing the company's advertising and sponsorships with media relations and financial public relations programmes.

The Air Canada case discussed earlier (see page 32) also provides an example of how well-managed public relations activities complement an organization's marketing objectives. Public relations activities – particularly involving media relations – are managed by Air Canada to develop the reputation of the airline as safe and reliable and able to provide the public services of air transportation. Developing and sustaining the company's reputation assists the company to market its services.

In another airline example, British Airways has used public relations and internal communication techniques to bring about change in the organization over recent years, to improve the company's approach to customer service, to support the company's move into the private sector, and to help the company through the acquisitions that have been made to increase the airline's size and competitiveness.

Whereas, in the case of Dunhill, public relations staff report to the senior marketing manager, in both Air Canada and British Airways there are substantial public affairs and public relations departments which collaborate with marketing staff.

Public relations as a corrective to the marketing approach

As a corrective to the marketing approach, public relations introduces another perspective into management decision-making. There are examples of products whose safety has been called into question, but which have been allowed to remain on the market as a result of management decisions which though they have weighed commercial and marketing considerations, have not taken into account effects of public doubt on the long-term interests and reputation of the organizations concerned. Public relations can introduce these elements into management decision-making – if public relations advisers are part of, or have access to the management decision-making group.

A good recent example of where public relations advice might have had this impact is to be found in the case of Suzuki and the problems that the company encountered with its four-wheel drive vehicle, the Samurai, which some tests showed had a tendency to overturn at slow cornering speeds. The problems were described by the *Washington Post*, in a report published on June 16, 1988, as constituting a classic management crisis, in which the reputation of the corporation was threatened by questions about the integrity of its product.

The Consumers' Union – a national consumer interest group – and later the Consumers' Association in the United Kingdom both questioned the safety of the vehicle, but the company opted for an aggressive defence of the product arguing that it was safe and stable. In the United States, the company added to its advertising campaign, with advertisements which affirmed that the Samurai was safe and reliable.

The aim of the company's defence was to protect the position of the product in the market place, but the criticism levelled at the company was that it was not doing enough to allay public concern for the safety of its products. Commentators with expertise in crisis management and public relations said at the time that the company should have collaborated with its critics to address public safety concerns, rather than attacking them.

The reaction of Suzuki can be contrasted with that of Perrier, mentioned earlier (see Chapter 1 page 14). Even though levels of contamination of Perrier's product were low and harmless, the company chose to respond to public concern by withdrawing the product from sale until the source of contamination had been identified and removed. The company emerged from a period of absence from the market with its reputation secure and enhanced by its speedy response to public concern about its products.

Decisions regarding product recall do involve the likelihood of large losses for the organization concerned. Simon Caulkin,[4] writing on Perrier's handling of the crisis it faced, suggests that the total cost of the contamination of Perrier's product will not be known for months or perhaps years to come, but the company faced the costs involved in lost sales, disposal of the recalled product and relaunching Perrier water on to the world market.

These decisions are clearly not decisions that can be made lightly, but they are better for having information and advice from public relations practitioners fed in to them. In the Perrier case, the company's management of the product recall in the United Kingdom was guided by a four-person disaster team consisting of the chairman, the marketing director and their public relations and advertising advisers.

The public relations perspective is likely to become increasingly important in management decision-making in coming years, as broad social concerns, for example for the state of the environment or for the safety of industrial processes, have to be taken into account as decisions are made.

Marketing communications and public relations

Some confusion of marketing and public relations activities arises because both marketing and public relations make use of communication to pursue their objectives. The traditional marketing view is that public relations is a form of communication and that it fits into the communication mix available to marketers as they promote goods and services. We've already looked at the arguments for a broader view of public relations, suggesting that it involves more than communication. It does, though, involve managed communication and the techniques it uses are similar to those used in marketing communications.

Marketing communications includes forms and techniques of communication which support the marketing and promotion of products and services, such as advertising, techniques of communication at point of sale and product publicity. Public relations uses communication to build, sustain and influence relationships. The distinction becomes difficult to see when marketing communications activities are directed at promoting particular products with potential customers, and public relations activities are in place to help build relations with potential customer groups. It is, nevertheless, there, and the consequences of the distinction have to be managed: for example, who should manage marketing communications? Should a marketing department have control over other communications activities aimed at customers?

Techniques of communication available to both marketing and public relations include:

- *Advertising.* In marketing, advertising is used specifically to support and promote specific goods and services in the market-place. In public relations, advertising is used to present images of a particular organization, or to make the organization's case, as in advocacy advertising, in order to affect perceptions of the organization and the way people relate to it. In some advertising, it is possible to see marketing and public relations purposes being served, for example in current advertising by banks, which though it points to services offered, also suggests that the relationship of the bank to its customers has changed and that the bank has become friendlier and more accessible

■ *Mass media techniques*. In marketing, approaches are made to the media (newspapers, radio and television), in order to generate publicity for products and services. Editorial mention of a product is more credible than advertising. Publicity, mention of products, goods and services in the news and feature columns of newspapers, magazines and trade publications, becomes an aim of marketing communications activity.

Some of public relations' poor reputation can be attributed to the mistaken labelling of marketing communications activity as public relations. A complaint raised by journalists and editors that copy provided in product press releases is copy that should be in advertisements, and paid for, is a complaint that should be directed against marketing communication, which is promotional, rather than against public relations, which has other objectives. Public relations and the media were discussed in Chapter 2, but the aim in public relations is to work with the media, and media personnel, to provide information and to ensure accurate and, as far as possible, sympathetic, coverage

■ *Promotional materials*, such as publications, brochures, videos, or displays. These can be used in marketing communication at point of sale, and to support the work of sales staff. In public relations, the same materials can be used to present a company's position, for example at a series of public meetings, or to explain a company's aims and objectives to its own employees, as in the Prudential case we looked at earlier (see page 40)

■ *Interpersonal communication*. Face-to-face communication is used in marketing communication at exhibitions, or by members of a company's sales force. It can take the form of a sales presentation made by an individual, or formal presentations made in front of small or large groups of people. In public relations practice, presentations or speeches may be made in front of groups of people to win understanding for a company's objectives and activities. This is not an exhaustive list of examples

In practice, marketing communication and public relations activities can interweave and be complementary, but they need to be carefully managed to achieve results against an organization's marketing and public relations objectives.

Conflict in marketing and public relations management

One obstacle to the effective management of marketing and public relations activities together is found in the conflict that may develop between marketing and public relations staff. In one large multinational high technology company that I studied recently conflict between marketing and public relations staff led to the following sequence of events. The company's United Kingdom subsidiary, in itself a major company in the United Kingdom, had a marketing department, which included marketing communications, community relations, internal communications and public affairs sections. Conflict between staff involved in public relations tasks and marketing staff led to the public relations staff breaking away to form a separate public relations department, which included marketing communications. This section still worked closely with the marketing department.

There followed a period of unproductive conflict between the former marketing department and the new public relations department, with both groups competing to demonstrate the value of their services to the organization to senior management. The public relations department worked in the areas of public affairs, community relations and internal communication, as well as providing marketing communications support to the marketing department. At the end of this period of conflict, the difficulties between the two departments were dealt with in a decision by senior management that the two departments should re-unite, with public relations activities re-absorbed into the marketing department.

One solution to conflict of this kind is to treat public relations as a part of marketing activities – Kotler's solution – and manage public relations through a senior manager responsible for marketing. This is the approach taken in the Dunhill case examined earlier (see page 67). This approach may only serve to bring conflict between marketing and public relations staff into the marketing department.

There are some good reasons for the conflict, some of which we have already referred to as having to do with the different perspectives of marketing and public relations. Marketing is the more established function, and has been in the ascendant as an overall approach to management in recent years. Public relations is at the same stage now in its development as marketing was 20 years ago.

Marketing is a more precise practice, which is able to draw on research as it manipulates a small number of variables to aim for predicted results, such as sales targets and measurable market share. Public relations is, at present, much less likely to be based on research. Although it should be a research-based practice, clients for public relations services do not see it as such and practitioners themselves are not trained in the use of research techniques. Public relations is concerned with a far larger number of variables – the attitudes, opinions and behaviour of a large number of groups – and the organization's whole presentation of itself to those groups. Public relations is also oriented to the future, and to identifying possible disruptions to important relationships. Marketing is also concerned with the future, but the marketing conception of the future is one based on extrapolations of trends in consumption, lifestyles and attitudes. It is arguably a narrower conception than the view of the world required in public relations.

It is more difficult to identify the results of public relations activities. Marketing activities can be correlated with improvements in sales figures or with growth in market share. Public relations activities may result in a series of events not happening, or decisions not being made. The results of public relations activities can be traced back to the activities themselves, but with more difficulty.

The seeming imprecision of public relations practice lays practitioners open to criticism from marketers, and also strengthens the latters' claim to manage public relations activities. What needs to be appreciated about public relations is that its imprecision, properly managed, is what makes the practice valuable! A study by Keegan in 1974[5] which examined the way senior managers in multinational companies gather information about the environment for use in making decisions found that public relations practitioners are good sources of information because they hear so much. Even if they are not directly involved, they are on the grapevine for information. An effective public relations practitioner is in contact with many sources of information, formally and informally, through research or through personal contacts.

Another reason for conflict between marketing and public relations is what has sometimes been called 'marketing imperialism.' Marketing, as an ascendant function whose importance is unquestioned, takes in all other areas of management, according to this view. Marketing helps the organization to adjust its productive capacity to the needs and wants of the society it serves, marketing interprets the environment, marketing ensures that the organization remains close to its customers, and so on. Marketing becomes the driving force of management, if this approach is taken to its extreme, and is resented by others in its ascendancy, not least by public relations staff who are able to see the limitations of the marketing approach. This could not, for example, cope with the aftermath of the Exxon Valdez oil spill disaster in Alaska recently.

One answer to the problem of marketing imperialism is to see marketing in more realistic terms, and to acknowledge the limitations of the marketing approach, as well as its obvious strengths and benefits.

Another reason for conflict between marketing and public relations staff follows from a principle of public relations practice which has sometimes difficult practical consequences. To be of most value, public relations advisers should be able to provide their advice to the most senior levels of management in the organizations in which, or for which they are working. If they are not reporting to the most senior levels of management, then they have to manoeuvre to a position where they are able to provide advice directly to senior management. If they are located in marketing departments where the senior marketing manager is not fully aware of the contribution public relations can make, they will be obliged to bypass the senior marketing manager and provide information directly to senior management. In many organizations, senior managers recognize their need to have direct contact with their public relations staff and establish direct or indirect reporting relationships so that public relations staff can work with them on a regular basis.

The driving principle of public relations practice, that advice should be given at the highest level of the organization, may lead to conflict between public relations managers seeking to provide their advice at the senior level, and others who stand in the way of such direct contact. If public relations is conceived of as marketing support, then efforts by public relations staff to report to senior management on developing issues, on matters of corporate image, community or government relations, or crisis management will be seen as outside the scope of public relations – and yet will be vitally important to the organization.

Conflict between marketing and public relations may be beneficial to the organization, because out of conflict reasons for advice given and actions recommended will be more keenly argued. But there is the danger that the conflict might prove to be unproductive. The task of the senior manager with responsibility for staff working in both marketing and public relations is to be aware that the conflict can occur, and that it must be managed.

Summary points

Public relations is viewed by many as part of marketing, but is a broader management task. It shares some similarities with marketing: both involve similar processes, and both make use of communication. Marketing has been seen as the central management task in recent years, concerned ideally with providing benefits to consumers and with finding, satisfying and maintaining and building positions in markets. Public relations is a complementary practice, which may also act as a corrective to the marketing approach. It should – although writers like Philip Kotler have argued otherwise – be separate from marketing, able to provide its perspective direct to senior management and also able to negotiate, rather than have enforced, its collaboration with marketing. In practice, a number of ways of managing the two functions are possible, and organizations will work through to the most suitable arrangements, but only by being fully aware of what should be expected from both functions.

CHAPTER EIGHT

CRISIS MANAGEMENT

ONE OF THE areas of management in which public relations has staked out a special interest and developed real expertise in recent years is that of crisis management. There are some good reasons for this: a crisis, emergency or disaster is usually a very public event, and the performance of any organization caught in crisis is subject to immediate public scrutiny as it tries to deal with the many consequences of a crisis situation. The organization's performance at such a time will be remembered, and in some cases memories of how poorly it responded may, sooner or later, contribute to driving it out of existence.

A crisis for any organization involves a serious threat to its interests and existence, with which it has to deal quickly, in order to minimise its consequences. Managers making decisions within an organization in crisis are subjected to high levels of stress, as they are forced to take decisions under time pressure, often with insufficient information. A crisis may be an emergency, for example, a mining accident in which there is limited time to rescue trapped personnel, a disaster such as the Zeebrugge ferry sinking, when a cross-channel ferry rolled over shortly after leaving the Belgian port of Zeebrugge and a large number of passengers lost their lives, or some other threatening situation such as an unexpected takeover bid made upon an unsuspecting company.

Public relations helps to manage important relationships at time of crisis, by paying close attention to communication and to the way information about the crisis is managed. Its contribution is in sustaining important relationships, for example with employees and their families, the media and the general public, through the crisis and its aftermath, and meeting public interests as well as those of the organization itself. Public relations at time of crisis contributes to helping to maintain the organization's reputation through the crisis, which is partly achieved by the way the organization responds, and is seen to respond, to public and special group interests.

Public relations has come to play a central role in crisis management, to the extent that crisis management is now one of public relations' most prominent contributions to management. In dealing with crisis its contribution is made at three stages. First, public relations is an anticipatory practice, and can assist in crisis planning, the efforts made by organizations to predict and prepare for possible crises. Second, public relations is an important part of the overall management task at time of crisis. Finally, it has a contribution to make to dealing with the aftermath of crisis.

Crisis planning

Crises, by definition, are unexpected. Organizations are pushed into crisis by the unexpected threat, emergency or disaster. In a comprehensive study of the Japanese surprise attack on Pearl Harbor in 1941, Roberta Wohlstetter[1] showed that, even when an organization with the resources of the United States government and armed forces has tried to plan for all eventualities, surprise, or the unexpected, is still possible. Planning for possible crisis situations is an important preparation, and when events occur which fit the plans that have been made, the organization can respond efficiently and well.

Planning for crisis involves thinking the unthinkable. What is the worst that can befall the organization? For some organizations, developing a list of things that can go wrong is a relatively easy task, if time and managerial attention is devoted to it. Even so, recent disasters have shown that predictable events can pitch the organizations experiencing them into crisis. The Zeebrugge ferry disaster caught the ferry company by surprise: some telling television news coverage of the company's reaction found its information officer responding to public enquiries about the disaster by noting queries received on the back of a newspaper! As Roberta Wohlstetter pointed out in her assessment of the reaction of US armed forces to the Pearl Harbor attack, it is possible to assess the extent to which an organization is surprised by the activities of its staff. One of the signs that an organization has been surprised is the extent to which its members are *caught* doing normal, everyday things.

Public relations' contribution to crisis planning is to help the organization and its senior managers to consider what might go wrong. Public relations, as we have seen earlier in this book, is an anticipatory practice that tries to foresee trends, events and issues which may arise to disrupt important relationships. Its monitoring activities, informal contacts and range of contacts all add to its usefulness as a part of crisis planning. Some examples:

- A public relations practitioner working for a pharmaceutical company that is known to test some of its products using live animals might monitor the activities and public statements of animal rights campaigners, to assess their militancy and to help in planning by the company to prepare for possible action by extremists on company facilities or personnel
- Concerns for food safety might be monitored by a public relations department to help a food manufacturer prepare for a drastic fall off in demand for its products as a result of food scares (for example, the recent strong public reactions in the United Kingdom to fears about salmonella in eggs and the possible effects of 'mad cow disease' on the safety of beef for human consumption)
- A company concerned that it might be a potential target for a takeover bid might expect its public relations department to monitor and report on shareholder opinion

and commentary on the company's performance in the financial press and among important interest groups

Practical obstacles to crisis planning are that it is time-consuming, and its relevance to the immediate day-to-day requirements of running a business or other organization will probably not be recognized – until a crisis occurs. A task for public relations is to keep raising questions regarding the organization's preparedness for crisis.

Crisis plans, once made, do need to be kept up to date, and the actions they involve should be rehearsed. One organization for which I worked some years ago in western Canada had a thoroughly developed set of plans for natural disasters such as forest fires and severe floods, which frequently occurred in the region. Unfortunately, the plans depended on named individuals being available to play certain roles at time of disaster, but the plans were not revised to keep up with staff changes, and when fires or floods occurred plans had to be re-made before the organization could respond. Failure to keep plans up-to-date slowed the organization's response, and also meant that hasty decisions at time of disaster might result in the assignment of the wrong staff to key roles.

Rehearsal of actions called for in plans can pay great dividends at time of crisis, particularly if actual events are close to events used as a basis for rehearsal. Emergency services now regularly carry out realistic simulations of predictable disasters such as train or aircraft crashes. In these simulations, public relations staff manage public information requirements, and have the opportunity to test channels of communication.

Practical approaches to crisis planning might involve a group of senior managers considering the very need to plan for crisis and the nature of events which might befall the organization. Planning starts with the asking of a series of 'what if?' questions, and considering, in imagination, series of actions which might follow from the answers to the questions.

An example might be a social services organization, or a commercial organization, providing residential care for the elderly. What if something went badly wrong with the quality of care provided? For example, what if standards of food preparation slipped, and food poisoning in one of the residential homes affected all the residents, or caused some of them to die? What can the organization do now to avoid such a development, and what would it do if it occurred? What if the standard of facility management declined, and resulted in some facilities becoming unsafe, or at worst becoming fire hazards? What if a fire broke out in one of the facilities, resulting in loss of life?

This process of questioning leads to a list of potentially critical events or developments which the organization could face. The organization's possible response can then be worked through, to see what it might do and who might have responsibility for various aspects of its response. This is an exercise in imaginative thinking, projecting a sequence of events into the future, to see what might happen. In the example just considered, the social services or commercial organization offering residential care for the elderly might decide, after reviewing its safety rules and current fire precautions, that the possibility of fire still existed. It could then imagine the kinds and severity of fire which might occur, and examine how the organization would deal with the consequences if one broke out.

This exercise could involve considerable attention to detail: how would the fire be discovered? Who would raise the alarm? What arrangements would be in place to ensure a safe evacuation of the facility? How would emergency services gain access to the site? What arrangements would the organization need to make to manage the situation, and who would be involved? How would the organization cope with enquiries from relatives, the media and others? Who would speak for the organization, what information would they be able to release, and at what point? Would the organization have in place the necessary means of communication? For example, would telephone lines into the facility remain intact and would they be sufficient in number to deal with telephone enquiries, or would additional lines, or some alternative information point need to be established?

This exercise of thinking through potential responses to crisis, far from being a waste of management time, helps to uncover inadequacies in present arrangements, as well as laying the basis for plans to deal with possible crises. In the example, thinking about the possibility of fire might raise questions about current evacuation plans.

Public relations' contribution to crisis planning in this example might be to raise the whole question in the first place. What would the consequences for the organization and its reputation be if a fire occurred at one of its facilities? The organization exists to provide safe, reliable care for the elderly, and important groups would need to be reminded, continually, that care embodying these standards was being provided. Important groups would include: residents and potential residents, their families, groups and individuals providing support to the facilities involved, such as government funding bodies, and the general public. Anything which might call into question the safety of the facilities would damage relations with these groups.

If, despite all precautions, a fire did break out, public relations would be involved in providing information about the situation to the same groups, and would have a role in dealing with enquiries from the media. These tasks would need to be thought out carefully before the event, so that responsibilities for speaking to the media and for making sure that relatives and other key groups were kept informed would be established.

Management at time of crisis

Management at time of crisis is management under conditions of stress. A crisis will distort the routine processes of decision-making in an organization. Although communication increases with more information coming into the organization and more going out, decisions are made in haste by a small group of people, who have to base them on incomplete information.

Information is incomplete partly because, even though more information is available, there is insufficient time to process and interpret it. Under such conditions, there is ample scope for poor decisions to be made, and for errors which can return to haunt the group making them when circumstances return to normal.

An example of the stress felt by senior executives is shown in the reaction of Sotheby's chief executive when, as we saw in Chapter 1, the company was threatened with an unfriendly takeover in 1983 by an organization based in the United States. Although the bid had been rumoured for some months, when it came it caught the Sotheby's senior management group by surprise. The bid was ultimately unsuccessful, but in the stress of the first few days after it was made the company's chief executive was reported in *The Sunday Times*[2] to have said that he would blow his brains out if the bid was successful. He was not, the report went on to suggest, the only one at the company to 'lose his cool.'

One of the important requirements for effective crisis management is awareness of the limitations on decision-making at time of crisis. Efforts have to be made to reduce the stress on decision-makers, and to bring the flow of information into and from the organization under control.

Michael Regester, one of the UK public relations practitioners who have established themselves as experts in crisis management, has set out a number of practical pointers to setting up an effective crisis management decision-making unit in his book on crisis management.[3] He emphasizes the need to reduce pressure on the key decision-makers by providing them with a number of rooms, an emergency centre or 'war room', from which they can work to manage the crisis. These rooms become the centre of flows of information about the crisis. All information about the situation can be fed into the groups of people working in these rooms, for interpretation and decision-making. Information out can also be managed, and named spokesmen and women can brief the media in a suitable nearby facility. These rooms have to be equipped with adequate communinications: sufficient telephone, fax, telex and other communications links.

In a crisis the immediate task will be to respond to the demands of the situation that has developed. For example, there may be casualties to evacuate or rescue, specific groups of people to be informed urgently of the dangers of consequences of the situation, a need to organize resources to overcome the situation that has developed, or all of these tasks and more to be carried out immediately. Public relations' contribution at this time in the management of a crisis situation is to:

- Help to reduce the stress experienced by, and unnecessary demands made upon, senior management faced with making decisions on the handling of the crisis. This can be done by public relations staff providing brief but accurate reports on the requirements for information of key groups, such the media, employees and relatives
- Assist in setting up and staffing the emergency centre, with trained public relations staff able to advise on response to requests for information and relations with the media
- Begin to gather already prepared background information on the organization for distribution to the media and other interested groups. Michael Regester emphasizes the importance of releasing information of this type as soon as possible, to demonstrate a willingness to communicate and also to begin to provide information to fill an early demand for it until more details of the crisis situation become available
- Ensure that all communication from the organization demonstrates that it is in control of the situation, as far as possible
- Ensure that the organization is shown to be concerned about the human consequences of the situation

Public relations plays a critical part in the early management of crisis situations. For example, when a British Midland Boeing 737 crashed on the M1 motorway in the English Midlands in 1989, the company's chairman, Michael Bishop, won admiration for his company's response to the disaster through his willingness both to speak for the company and to provide information on what had occurred on the flight. By acting as company spokesman, and fulfilling a public relations role, linking the company to key groups directly and through the media, he demonstrated the company's concern for what had happened.

Well-managed public relations activities at the time of crisis enable the organization dealing with the crisis to demonstrate to important groups that it is coping with the crisis and deserving of public sympathy and support, as the case of Johnson and Johnson[4] in the United States shows. When the company was faced with a number of deaths as a result of deliberate contamination of one of its major products, Tylenol, with cyanide, it responded with a total withdrawal of the product from the market. The withdrawal and subsequent relaunch of a 'tamper-proof' Tylenol on the market were accompanied by precisely-targeted communication directed at groups such as doctors, hospitals and distributors. The company was able to recapture most of the market share it had had for the product before the crisis shortly after the product was re-launched. It did so partly because it was able to show by its actions that it was prepared to suffer considerable loss to ensure public safety and that it deserved public sympathy and support.

Managing the aftermath of crisis

How an organization manages public relations at the time of crisis can also have longer-term consequences as it deals with the aftermath. The public stance of the organization at the time of crisis will be remembered, and may even be cited as evidence against it, if the crisis results in some form of public enquiry being established to look into its causes. The organization which tries, while dealing with the crisis, to deny responsibility for its consequences before evidence has been weighed, or which fails to demonstrate concern for people who may have suffered as a result of the crisis, may find it has little support or sympathy from the public when it comes to look for it again.

Once the crisis is over, once decisions have been made and actions taken which resolve the crisis, the task of dealing with the aftermath remains. In the aftermath, the organization may have to work to restore confidence in its operations, or to regain its credibility. In some cases, this cannot be done. The organization which is so damaged by the events of the crisis, or which behaved during the crisis so poorly that public confidence is lost, may not be able to regain public support and may be forced out of existence.

In other cases, for example, Johnson and Johnson's or Perrier's, the crisis may be followed by an aftermath which presents the organization with a number of opportunities to strengthen its position. Johnson and Johnson were able to relaunch a product which met consumer concerns about safety with a new tamper-proof capsule. Perrier were able to reintroduce their mineral water into a market in which sympathy for the company, and an appreciation of the way the company had dealt with the contamination of its product, had been generated.

Public relations activities can be managed during the aftermath of a crisis to try to repair the damage that has been done to the organization, or to capitalize on the opportunities the crisis has thrown up. Where damage has been serious, the task of public relations will be to help in rebuilding relationships and reputation. This will be a long-term task and may end in failure. In the case of the company which operated the ill-fated Zeebrugge ferry, *The Herald of Free Enterprise*, the company ceased to exist as a separate corporate entity and was absorbed into its parent company. The long-term rebuilding task taken on by other organizations involves addressing defects in performance and then informing important groups at every opportunity that the problems which gave rise to the crisis or disaster have been addressed.

Managing public relations for crisis management

If public relations is to make its contributions to crisis planning, to crisis management, and to dealing with the aftermath of crisis, senior management groups must establish and staff the function so that it can make these contributions. Public relations staff or the organization's public relations group should be in a position to provide advice and contribute to planning for crises. For example, if an organization can foresee that it might be the subject of an unwanted takeover bid, it should include public relations staff in planning to defend itself.

Public relations staff should be given responsibility for developing plans for dealing with the public relations aspects of crises. An airline can expect that at some time one of its aircraft will suffer some mishap. All aspects of an aircraft crash can be planned for, and simulated, including requirements for dealing with media interest and informing relatives and others of developments.

Senior management should also recognize that public relations involves looking to the future, and to events which may arise to disrupt relationships. Staff appointed to public relations positions should be selected for their foresight and judgement, and encouraged to use their abilities in developing crisis plans for the organization. Senior management may not have time to develop crisis plans, but they will need to delegate this task to staff who can return to them with workable schemes. We will return to the qualities to be looked for in public relations staff in Chapter 11.

Crisis plans can be checked in practice through simulations, or in discussions with groups whose cooperation will be needed to put them into effect. Public relations staff contacts with groups such as media personnel can be used to set up discussions of plans and their practicality. The role of the media in crisis management can be overlooked in crisis planning, with disastrous effects at time of crisis. Michael Regester[5] illustrates this point to great effect in presentations on crisis management by showing news coverage of a press conference at which a hapless chief executive officer shows that he is not prepared for questioning by journalists after a disaster on an oil rig in the North Sea. By working with the media at the crisis planning stage, their expectations for information at time of crisis can be met – within limits, which can be explored at the crisis planning stage, rather than discovered when the crisis occurs.

Public relations staff can also help in training other staff and senior management for their parts in managing crisis, for example by training senior managers to be able to respond to journalists' questions at time of crisis.

Checklists for managing public relations for crisis management

Crisis planning

- Senior management should expect their public relations staff – inside or outside the organization – to have the skills, foresight, judgement and contacts to make a major contribution to crisis planning
- Senior management should be able to delegate the task of crisis planning to public relations and other staff groups, who should then return with workable crisis plans
- Public relations staff should be able to draw on their contacts – with the media, interest groups, the community and community organizations – to be able to test both the plans they have made and the communication links they involve
- Public relations staff should have sufficient credibility with management groups within the organization to be able to provide, or procure, training for crisis management – and to persuade managers to take part in the training

Crisis management

At time of crisis, senior managers should look to public relations staff to help 'take the pressure off', by helping to set up systems for managing flows of information about the situation into and from the organization, and by working directly with important groups such as the news media.

In the aftermath of crisis

In the aftermath of a crisis, public relations activities are directed towards rebuilding relationships and the organization's position. Senior managers should expect to make realistic plans for these activities and well-managed allocation of resources to them.

Crisis management – summary points

Crisis management is an area of special expertise within public relations practice, which is oriented towards the future, and towards trying to anticipate events which may disrupt important relationships. Public relations practice has an important contribution to make to crisis planning, crisis management itself, and to dealing with the aftermath of crisis. The experience of recent years, which have produced a number of widely-publicized disasters – many of them international in their impact – suggests that we can expect regular occurrence of natural and man-made disasters. In the business world, the pressures of world-wide competitive forces will create more threatening situations for many companies. These trends suggest that public relations' part in management will increase in importance, because of its developing role in crisis management.

CHAPTER NINE

PUBLIC RELATIONS AND CORPORATE CULTURE

EFFECTIVE PUBLIC RELATIONS practice, which contributes to the achievement of management objectives and to organizational cohesiveness, survival and prosperity, depends on accurate social analysis. This analysis involves understanding how groups outside the organization – government, pressure groups, the media and community organizations, for example – relate to each other, and how the organization itself works, as a collection of groups, such as management and employees, or professional and unionized staff, or generalists and specialists. Underlying social analysis and understanding there should be an appreciation of culture, the pattern of beliefs, attitudes, opinions, basic assumptions and habitual practices which marks one cultural group from another in the wider society and in the organization itself.

It is only quite recently that managers have come to accept the idea that organizations themselves, like nations and societies, have cultures, and that within organizations separate cultural groups, sub-cultures, can be identified. Widely-read, popular management books such as Peters and Waterman's *In Search of Excellence*[1] pointed to the importance of organizational culture in determining whether or not an organization is successful.

Newer approaches to management problems, such as Organization Development (OD), take as their starting point the idea that culture can be changed in order to deal with problems and to help organizations achieve their objectives. As Geert Hofstede[2] has pointed out, behaviour in organizations is strongly influenced by organizational culture. If managers want to try to change the behaviour of organization members, one way to do this is through attempts to change organizational culture.

A good example of this approach at work is to be found in organizations now trying to change the way in which they treat their customers, through customer care progammes. British Airways, for example, recently carried out a comprehensive and effective customer care programme to change the attitudes and behaviour of staff towards customers. In order to do this, the belief that customer needs are of paramount importance has first to be established.

Public relations overlaps with organizational development work as organizations try to modify their own cultures. One of the main tasks of management is to point out to organization members what is important in their membership of the organization and in the work that they do within and for the organization. In this, managers are assisted by staff from personnel and public relations, among others. Personnel departments will develop position descriptions, describe conditions of employment, make available details of collective agreements and so on, while public relations staff will help in developing management messages for inclusion in internal newsletters, or in videos to be used for staff briefings.

Cultural values and meanings are communicated through the use of symbols, language and behaviour – even through the work environment itself. Public relations practice, as we've seen, makes use of communication to assist in the achievement of organizational objectives. It has a special interest in managed use of symbols and language, and this interest now extends into considering their use in developing organizational culture, climate and effectiveness.

Management interest is in seeing employees motivated and productive, and loyal to the organization, its values and objectives. Public relations' contribution is to employee communication and to the presentation of messages which will help to motivate and involve. Messages can be presented in a number of ways:

- *Through the work environment itself.* The organization which allows its employees to work in poor surroundings is communicating a number of messages to its employees, one of the worst of which is: we don't really care about your working conditions – or you. Part of public relations' task in internal communication is to ask what the physical environment in which people are asked to work 'says' to them, and to recommend improvements. If the organization lacks resources to improve the working environment, then efforts to explain this to employees should be made
- *Through signage and symbols in the working environment.* The impression of management created by these should not be overlooked. Well thought out systems of signage and good use of symbols make it easier for visitors to find their way into the organization's work areas, and also make it clear to staff what the areas are to be used for. Large established organizations, like IBM, or major hospitals make good use of signage and symbols in their builings and deliver strong messages to employees and visitors at the same time. Public relations' interest in signage is sometimes seen as a preoccupation with what other managers may regard as trivial detail, but being able to find a way through a strange organization's buildings is not a trivial matter for visitors or potential customers
- *Through artifacts used in, or produced by the organization.* Artifacts – things used or made by people – also express organizational values, perhaps embodying quality or modernity as key values. Artifacts might include furniture chosen for staff offices, stationery and pens provided to staff, or crockery used in a staff restaurant. All these items, and there are many other examples, make a statement about the organization and its values. They can also be used to build loyalty among organization members: for example, items of clothing marked with company symbols or badges can be made available to employees or others to

show their membership of and role in the organization. Public relations staff have an interest in the way artifacts are chosen and used, since they do make an important statement about the organization. A good example is provided by the company Christmas card: public relations staff will often be involved in recommending and choosing a suitable card which, at the same time as conveying Christmas or seasonal greetings, will say something about the values of the organization that is sending it

- *Through ritual.* Rituals involve ceremonies and rites of passage, such as retirement parties. Organizations develop their own rituals over time. For example, universities have formal convocations, at which graduates receive their graduation diplomas, companies have their annual meetings, social events or ceremonies to celebrate events of significance. To these rituals, public relations brings a shaping influence, for example to ensure maximum publicity within the organization for a retirement party, or to ensure that prominent members of the local community are invited to celebrations at the opening of a new company facility

- *Through language.* As Geert Hofstede suggests, language is the vehicle of culture and the way we think depends on the words we have at our disposal. Managers use language to give instructions, to motivate and persuade, but the language they use will be one which is distinctive to management and to the organization in which it is being used. Certain abbreviations, phrases and technical terms will carry meanings which may be unique to the organization. This language may require translation to convey concern or enthusiasm, or even to be understandable. The manager who uses the special language of jargon may require help in order to get his or her ideas across to a wider audience. The public relations practitioner is in a position to act as a translator, across organizational boundaries and between people in the same organization who use different languages. Acting in this way, the practitioner can act as a linchpin, helping to hold together different groups in the same organization

Public relations and organization development

Organization development, which is usually seen as a responsibility of personnel or human resource staff or departments, is a practice which sets out to bring about cultural change, to achieve some organizational objective – the solution of problems with staff morale and productivity, for example. The practice involves what are referred to as OD interventions to bring about change. These use a variety of techniques, research to understand problems or situations faced by the organization, and extensive work with groups of organization staff. Warren Bennis, who has written a number of books on organization development, has suggested that for an organization development project to be successful it must have the commitment of senior management, and must involve the intact work group – the group to be changed – or the whole organization if change is to be brought about in the organization.[3] Over half of the members of the group must be involved in the organization development project, and senior managers should also be included.

Organization development interventions focus on issues such as group integration, the development of effective work teams and the reduction of conflict; issues of group cohesion and effectiveness in which public relations also has an interest, but from a different perspective. Public relations can make a contribution to communication within the organization, and can assist efforts towards organization development. But it is also concerned with organization cohesion and consistency as the organization relates to its own members, and to groups outside.

Several years ago, I worked with a large British corporation that had recently reorganized to devolve responsibility for the several strands of the company's business activities to strategic business units. These units were given almost complete responsibility for their business activities and freedom to operate independently. The belief was that each unit would be more sensitive to its customer groups, and would be able to develop its activities as it saw fit. A small head office retained responsibility for overall financial control, strategic planning, some personnel and IT policies, and corporate communications for the company and its constituent units.

At the time I became involved, the company was concerned at some of the consequences of the reorganization. The separate units were pulling in different and contradictory directions, and sending mixed messages about the company as a whole to important groups such as politicians and civil servants, the City, financial analysts and journalists. From a public relations perspective, some means had to be found to encourage the newly-independent business units to collaborate in a programme of communications activities to ensure that messages from the organization were consistent and mutually reinforcing, and to demonstrate that it was a cohesive whole.

A solution to the problems of the reorganization was to be found in the development of a company culture which endorsed the independence of the units, valued links and collaboration between the separate business units, and allowed the company's head office to coordinate the company's communications activities. In this example, organization development interests would be in helping the organization to develop a culture which allowed the units to collaborate with each other, for the benefit of the company as a whole. Public relations' interests, on the other hand, were in helping the organization to hold together and to present itself consistently to important groups.

The overlap between public relations and organization development is one that can be exploited and managed. A senior management group considering internal problems of employee morale or high levels of absenteeism might ask personnel or OD staff to work with public relations staff to arrive at solutions. Both groups have contributions to make to the solution of organizational problems which call for cultural change.

Public relations, design and corporate identity

Another group of specialists with strongly developed interests in cultural change are designers – such as the London-based consultancies Wolff Olins, which is independent, and Sampson Tyrell, a member company of the WPP group, which also includes the advertising agency J. Walter Thompson and the world-wide public relations consultancy Hill and Knowlton. Wolff Olins' projects in recent years have included corporate identity projects for the Prudential Corporation, which was mentioned in Chapter 3, the British government's Department of Trade and Industry and the Metropolitan Police in London.

Corporate identity involves much more than design, although design makes an important contribution to corporate identity. Wally Olins,[4] the head of Wolff Olins, argues that corporate identity is the sum of the organization's presentation of itself: it includes the facilities occupied by the organization, the way they are kept and decorated, the manner in which staff greet visitors, and the climate that exists within an organization. It also depends on the way in which information is presented by the organization through publications, all forms of written, printed and visual material. It also extends to signage, to vehicle liveries, and to symbols used by the organization. Symbols used by the organization should express the core values.

Olins' company's projects with organizations such as the Department of Trade and Industry and the Metropolitan Police have changed the way in which these organizations have presented themselves to important groups and to the general public. In the case of the Metropolitan Police, the work involved in developing the force's new corporate identity was also intended to help the police to change the way in which they served the community. It was to bring about cultural change within the police service.

The work of designers on corporate identity is of obvious

interest to public relations practitioners, who collaborate closely with designers on corporate identity components of public relations programmes, internal and external. In the Prudential case we examined earlier in Chapter 3, the head of public affairs for the Prudential worked in partnership with Wolff Olins staff on the corporation's new corporate identity programme which, as we saw, had some definite objectives for change in the company.

The collaboration between public relations practitioners and designers may be difficult to put into effect. This is partly because finding designers who are compatible with public relations staff, senior management and the organization's staff may be hard. Public relations practitioners as well as senior management will need to be sure that the designers have the research and consultancy skills to be able to assess the organization's needs and values, and the design capability to be able to produce design solutions which express its values and identity imaginatively and powerfully.

Few organizations, even the largest, will support their own design staff, and a decision to work with designers will, for most organizations, mean working with outside staff. Organizations making frequent use of design help will need to know of designers available to them, and will come to know which designers are best able to meet organizational needs. For organizations making less frequent use of design advice, each new project may involve a search for help, which may be time-consuming.

Deciding on a new corporate identity

When should an organization consider developing a new corporate identity for itself? The decision to opt for a new corporate identity might follow from:

- Management recognition that the existing corporate identity no longer matches the organization and what it has become

- Desire on the part of the management group to use corporate identity as a means of stimulating change within the organization
- The existing corporate identity has a dated look, and needs to be brought up to date
- The organization has changed its name and is seeking to relaunch itself with a new name and corporate identity

The Prudential Corporation chose to change its corporate identity because its senior management group felt that the old identity did not reflect the corporation and its new status as a financial services company operating in a very competitive marketplace. It also used its new corporate identity to change staff perceptions of the company and to motivate them.

British Petroleum and ICI have both examined their corporate identities in recent years, and brought them up to date with minor modifications of the well-known elements of their corporate identity programmes. Woolworth Holdings' transformation into Kingfisher led the company to develop an entirely new corporate identity.

The process of developing a new corporate identity

Developing a new corporate identity is not simply a matter of changing a few visual representations of the organization, for example the organization's logo or symbol, and colour schemes for vehicles. Corporate identity, as Wally Olins makes clear, involves all aspects of the organization's representation of itself, to itself and to groups outside the organization.

From a management point of view, developing a new corporate identity involves:

- Determining that there is a real need for a new identity. Has the organization changed? Is the existing identity no longer appropriate? Would a new identity contribute to change within the organization or change in the way the organization is perceived outside, and would these changes be of measurable benefit to it? Is the existing identity still up-to-date, or does it make use of graphical devices or colours which are now dated? Can likely costs of developing and introducing a new corporate identity be justified?

- Appointing a group of people to work on the new corporate identity. This group should include the organization's senior public relations manager, or senior manager carrying responsibility for public relations, and representatives of the design group, or the designer, who will be working on the development of the new corporate identity. The group might also include the staff member who will have responsibility for introducing and 'policing' the new corporate identity, if this person is not the public relations manager

- Ensuring that this group reports back to senior management as the new corporate identity is developed, so that progress and concepts which emerge can be checked and approved. The group's work will involve an audit of current elements of the organization's corporate identity, such as signage, logos, use of design in publications, presentations and so on; research among organization members and outside groups to check current perceptions of the organization, its values, mission and objectives; the development of design approaches to the findings of the research, and the presentation of design concepts and recommendations for approval

- Approving, winning senior management support for, and overseeing the introduction of the new corporate identity. The majority or the most powerful and influential of the organization's senior management group will have to approve the new corporate identity, and be prepared to back it, since it will, in most cases, involve a major change for the organization and its members

- Introducing the new corporate identity. This requires a detailed timetable, with a launch event, and a programme for the introduction of the new identity. Use of the new identity should be governed by a comprehensive manual, which sets out how the visual elements of the new identity should be used – on stationery, publications, buildings and vehicles for example

Use of the elements of the new identity will be governed by the manual and will need to be checked by an individual named to be responsible for the corporate identity programme. Much of the impact of introducing a new corporate identity will be lost if the new identity is not properly introduced, launched and monitored in its use.

The new identity will, for some members of the organization, represent an unwanted change, and it will be resisted in a number of ways. Some members of the organization will want to remain with the old identity, others will resist the new or try to ignore the rules. For some time, the task of the corporate identity manager will be a difficult one, as support for the new identity is sought, and rule-breakers are dealt with firmly. The rules do have to be applied firmly because of the investment in the new identity, and because the impact and value of the new identity will be lost if members of the organization are able to ignore it and continue to represent the organization using the old identity.

The benefits from a new identity, well introduced and widely accepted within the organization, can be immediate. The organization attracts attention to itself and, if the new identity stimulates the imagination and interest of people inside and outside the organization, can gain recognition for the qualities and values inherent in the new identity. On recent experience, new corporate identities are almost always controversial and subject to critical comment. Wolff Olins' work for the Department of Trade and Industry was criticized as being more suitable for a 1950s jukebox, while BP and ICI were questioned for spending large amounts of money for what seemed like minor adjustments to elements of their existing corporate identity programmes.

Work on the corporate identity of an organiztion touches on

some of the deepest values held by members of the organization, and disrupts the familiar. It offers an opportunity to
senior managers to stimulate discussion about the organization's mission, values and objectives, but the process of
developing a new corporate identity needs careful management and commitment to change.

Public relations and the story of the organization

Corporate identity programmes provide one way of telling the
organization's story to catch the imagination of organization
members and groups outside it. Corporate identity expresses
the values and myths which underlie work in any organization
in a shorthand of recognizable symbols, myths, colours,
publications, and behaviours. Typically, public relations staff
are active in the development of corporate identity programmes and in seeing that they are put into effect, but they also
have other ways of telling their organization's stories.

In the organization's culture, one of the tasks of the public
relations practitioner is to tell stories about the organization, to
dramatize it for the benefit both of the people who make up
the organization and for outsiders. This is a task shared with
senior management, and evidence of the work done to
complete this task is found in in-house newspapers, in public
announcements by the organization's senior management and
in the scripts of video productions relating to the organization's
work. The stories told add to the organization's mythology and
become part of the culture, reinforcing and adding to it.

Culture has rational and irrational elements. This is brought
out well in an stimulating book by Graham Cleverley,[5] which
approaches management from the perspective of anthropol-
ogy, a branch of the social sciences which has made a special
study of primitive societies. More recently, the anthropological
perspective has been brought to bear on modern, industrial
societies and groups within them. Cleverley views managers as
a making up a group with its own subculture, and examines
some of the irrational beliefs and practices which are found

among managers as a group. These beliefs and practices are irrational in the sense that they are non-rational. They may be based upon faith, superstition or unexamined tradition, and they are a potent force in life in organizations. For example, it is not possible to foresee the future, yet managers put their faith in forecasting techniques which give them some confidence about the way in which the future is going to unfold.

Graham Cleverley's book suggests that the world outside the organization is an uncertain place, and that groups from the outside, like journalists, with an interest in what goes on within the organization, have to be kept at bay, which may be the task of the public relations practitioner. He compares the practitioner to the individual in the primitive tribe who has the task of keeping evil spirits in check. This is far less fanciful than it may seem. In my own experience, I have seen otherwise highly competent managers lose all their poise and confidence before entering interviews with journalists and have felt them looking to me, as a public relations practitioner, for help in taking on the threat that they felt that journalists represent.

Public relations practitioners and the managers with whom they work need to be aware of the emotional and irrational aspects of organizational culture, for a number of reasons. If they can appreciate, and work with, the organizational culture, then they can tap in to it to try to achieve organizational objectives. In the United States and Canada, payroll giving, a means by which employees can ask for deductions from their salaries to be made by employers for donations to charities, is well established, particularly through an annual campaign for donations to the United Way. The United Way is an umbrella organization that brings together charities for a common appeal to the public and to companies and other organizations. Each year it is a matter of some pride for each organization to try to exceed its previous year's collections for the United Way, and each year committees within organizations are set up to solicit donations from employees. These campaigns are most successful in organizations which already have a powerful commitment to community service as a belief embedded in their cultures. Culture, and the beliefs which make it up, contributes to the achievement of specific objectives.

Knowledge of organizational culture is also necessary so that plans or objectives which might run counter to beliefs and practices in the culture are not adopted, without thought on how they might be received, or on how the culture might have to change to make them acceptable. Sensitivity to organizational culture is required of all managers, but particularly from public relations practitioners.

Practitioners need to be aware also of their roles as organizational story tellers and contributors to the development and life of the organization's culture. They are often involved in putting into words or pictures some of the organization's stories and values, in a way which helps its members to make sense of the organization and their part in it. This was true in the Prudential case study: following the launch of the company's new corporate identity, at which explanations of the new identity and the company's future intentions were given, employees who attended were questioned and said that their understanding of the company had changed. They believed that the company had a new dynamism, and a clear sense of direction for the future. This reaction is quite common after staff have an opportunity to see a well-produced audio-visual presentation on some aspect of the work of their organization. A well-written script and strong images combine to present a dramatic picture of the organization, which can have a powerful impact on staff who may be seeing the organization in this way for the first time. As one staff member in an organization for which I developed an audio-visual presentation some years ago said, after seeing the result, 'I hadn't realised I worked for such an interesting organization.'

Story-telling and working to influence or change organizational culture raises some questions regarding the ethics of public relations practice. Story-telling may suggest to some people 'bending' or shaping the truth, but story-telling involves taking information about the organization and the people who are part of it and using it imaginatively, in ways which will spark interest and involvement. The same material can be used to produce a dry and factual report, or a feature article for a company newspaper which will have some human interest. Story-telling involves using the skills of the journalist and communicator to make information interesting, exciting or entertaining. Journalists do much the same thing: they gather information, and then write it or prepare it in a form that will be interesting to readers or viewers.

Ethically, public relations practitioners should be bound by codes of conduct which forbid the dissemination of information which is false or misleading. These codes are in place in most of the countries in which public relations is practised, but they are not universal in their application. It is important that practitioners, and the managers who work with them, do not abuse their insights into organizational culture. Change to organizational culture should be approached carefully and with sensitivity, not cynically and with intent to manipulate. Efforts to manipulate organizational culture may be discovered and resisted if they are covert, and resisted from the outset if they are overt.

My first experience of organization development was of an exercise that failed. It involved an attempt to integrate what had previously been a separate department of government into a larger department. OD techniques were used to try to change the beliefs held by members of the formerly independent department to bring them into line with the beliefs and attitudes of members of the new department. Members of the previously independent group resisted the overt attempt to bring about change and the exercise failed. The techniques and the management group which initiated them were discredited. Similar consequences can be expected for public relations activities aimed at having an effect on organizational culture if they are initiated with an intention to manipulate or mislead.

Joining the culture: public relations' contribution to socialization, orientation and training

Individuals join cultural groups by birth, involuntarily or by choice. Individuals are born into a national culture and learn its values, beliefs, ways of looking at world and behaving, through a process of socialization. They are socialized in family life, and through experiences at school and in other social groups. In a way, their socialization into a national society is involuntary, as it is for individuals who are required or forced to join organizations with strong internal cultures, such as the armed forces or prison.

Later in life, individuals choose to join organizations in which they find employment. They are socialized into these organizations in much the same way as they were socialised into their national society in early life. They have to learn the ways of the organization, and the organization makes certain opportunities available to them to learn about it and its values. The first such opportunity can be provided by an orientation or induction programme, which gives the individual a planned introduction to the organization and its practices. Later opportunities to learn more about the organization and its values are provided through training.

Public relations can make a number of contributions to helping the individual learn about the organization, through orientation and training programmes. Material about the organization can be produced to be sent to possible new entrants: for example, company information prepared in brochures or booklets for sending to new graduates to encourage them to apply for positions with the company. Similar material can be prepared for use in orientation and training programmes. This will probably be prepared through collaboraton between personnel and public relations staff, and will communicate some of the organization's values as well as factual information employees will need.

Culture as an asset

A strong organization culture, with values that are congruent with organizational objectives for productivity, customer service and employee satisfaction, is an asset. Just as attention is given to building and safeguarding other assets, attention should also be given to developing the organization's culture. This can be done by drawing out from the organization's members some of the values which guide their work, through research. It can also be done by working for agreement on a code of conduct which can guide employees, or for a 'mission statement' which encapsulates what the organization exists to achieve.

Public relations practitioners who use communication to establish relationships between the organization and important groups, including its own members, need to have a clear view of what the organization stands for, and what its underlying values are. They have an interest in making the organization's culture explicit and a role in developing and expressing the values, beliefs and attitudes which underlie its work. Their skills in communication put them in the position of being able to make sense of the organization, for groups outside it and for the organization itself. This ability is a relatively undeveloped aspect of the public relations practitioner's role, but one that will become more important as the work of modern organizations increases in complexity.

An example of this ability in use is found in the work of the public relations practitioner who is asked by a client to prepare a brochure which describes the client's organization, its objectives and services, for use with potential customers. The task itself is quite simple, and is one of the many technical jobs practitioners are called upon to perform. As the practitioner asks questions to begin putting material together, it becomes apparent that the client has not thought out, nor made clear either the organization's objectives, nor the reasons why certain services and not others are offered. The process of preparing the brochure helps to make sense of the organization, and the words chosen by the public relations practitioner help to explain the organization to itself. Comparable work may be carried out by the internal public relations practitioner asking questions about the organization's mission and objectives for publication and for use in communication with important groups.

Corporate culture – summary points

Cultural appreciation, the appreciation of the culture of the wider society and organizations within it, is essential in public relations practice and in management. Culture can be developed and changed to meet organizational objectives. Public relations can contribute to cultural change, working in collaboration with organization development, or alone. It can also contribute to activities aimed at developing new corporate identities for the organization, working in collaboration with designers. Using communication, public relations practice can dramatize organizational life, telling stories which emerge from and reinforce organizational culture. Its influence upon organizational or corporate culture raises questions about the ethics of the practice, which must avoid manipulation. Public relations practitioners can assist efforts to socialize new entrants into organizations, through orientation, induction and training programmes. Corporate culture is an asset which can be built and developed, but building culture as an asset depends on the devotion of adequate managerial attention to the task. Public relations, by providing this attention, can also help organizations understand themselves and their own cultures.

CHAPTER TEN

EVALUATING PUBLIC RELATIONS

A CURRENT CONCERN among public relations practitioners as a group is how to evaluate what they do, in terms that will be readily understood by clients and others. Public relations is an imprecise practice – earlier it was suggested that this is part of its value – but efforts have to be made to set precise, measurable objectives as a basis for activities, and for evaluation. Walter Lindenmann, a vice president of the New York consultancy, Ketchum Public Relations, has examined approaches to the evaluation of public relations activities over a number of years, and has concluded that the hunt for the best evaluation research techniques has yielded the cold, hard truth that public relations programmes are not easy to measure.[1]

Managers have a special interest in the evaluation of public relations activities, since it provides both an indication of whether or not they have produced results of real value and a guide in decisions about undertaking them. Evaluation helps to answer questions about the time, effort and resources to be invested in public relations activities: can the investment, and the costs involved, be justified?

Evaluation in public relations practice

Evaluation in public relations practice involves setting a value on public relations activities. This is done by measuring their effectiveness. If specific objectives are set for public relations activities, how effective is public relations in achieving those objectives? Evaluation looks back on activities, and examines results achieved against objectives and expenditure of time and effort.

The key to evaluation is research, a systematic gathering of information which can be used to help in setting objectives, assessing progress and weighing results. Burson-Marsteller, one of the largest of the US-headquartered world-wide public relations consultancies, has described three broad categories of research which can be used as an aid to evaluation:

- *Formative research*, which is carried out to help in programme development, to establish measures against which progress can be assessed and to refine objectives
- *Diagnostic research*, which is carried out during programme implementation to provide measures of progress, or to modify activities if necessary
- *Evaluative research*, which is carried to establish whether or not results have been achieved against objectives set

A communications audit may be used as formative research, to find out from employees and important publics how an organization is perceived, as a basis for developing a programme to change perceptions and the nature of the relationship between the organization and its publics.

Diagnostic research may be used in the early stages of a campaign to check that important messages are being received by target audiences. If they are not, modifications can be made to the programme. Dewe Rogerson, the UK consultancy which has developed campaigns to support the privatization of organizations such as British Gas, has made expert use of diagnostic research to shape the messages used at each stage of privatization, to communicate with and motivate potential shareholders. Evaluative research at the end of a series of activities may use surveys to find out if perceptions, attitudes and behaviour have changed as a result of the programme.

Evaluation may be based on formal research, but it can also draw on judgement and intuition, the importance of which in management should not be overlooked. If time and resources do not allow for elaborate evaluation, managers and practitioners will have to rely on judgement alone. But judgement should be checked against evidence as far as is possible. Evaluation can be a matter of 'disciplined intuition' in public relations, as much as in other areas of management.

Obstacles to evaluation in public relations

Obstacles to evaluation in public relations practice arise because of:

- Lack of time and resources for evaluation
- Lack of understanding of the scope of public relations
- Lack of understanding on the part of clients or management of the need for research and evaluation in public relations
- Lack of understanding on the part of practitioners of the role of research and evaluation in practice, and of techniques of research

Evaluation in public relations requires commitment of time and resources. In a busy public relations department, or in a small public relations consultancy, time and resources allocated to evaluation may be taken from time and resources available for developing new business, or managing continuing programmes. In public relations practice, cost of evaluation is a major obstacle to it. There is an acceptance on the part of clients for advertising services that the costs of research should be part of a proposal for expenditure on advertising, but research is not seen as an integral part of public relations activities and expenditure on it is agreed to only with great reluctance.

Evaluation is also time-consuming, since it depends on systematic attention to detail and to the gathering of information. Arrangements must be made for information to be gathered and interpreted. Information gathering for evaluation purposes is not activity which produces immediate results. Even though in the long term it improves the quality of programmes, in the short term it may be seen as a waste of time.

Another obstacle to evaluation in public relations practice is raised by lack of understanding on the part of managers and clients of the scope of public relations. They may not see public relations practice as one which lends itself to precise measurement. Some practitioners also believe that public relations, as a creative practice, cannot be evaluated using measures which might be appropriate in other areas of management. Managers and clients may have one of a number of conceptions of public relations, which may throw up obstacles to its evaluation:

- They may see it as a superficial and peripheral activity, to be carried on with minimum investment of time and resources
- They may see it as a marketing support activity, and assume that its contribution will be assessed at the same time as overall marketing activities are evaluated
- They may view the practice as one concerned only with communication, for example through the media, and look for communication output, such as news coverage, as an indication of effectiveness
- They may see the practice as an effort to generate goodwill and understanding, and evaluate it according to whether or not attitudes have changed among important groups

Each of these perceptions provides a partial view of public relations, which is not simply a marketing support activity, or communication, or an exercise in trying to generate goodwill. Certainly, evaluation can be applied in these areas, but it will be a partial evaluation.

By some clients and managers, public relations practice is seen as one to which research does not apply. Its role is established in marketing and advertising, but at this stage in the development of public relations practice research is not seen as important or necessary – although a research study completed recently by Walter Lindenmann suggests that, in the United States perceptions of the value of research are changing.[2]

A large obstacle to evaluation is raised by public relations practitioners' own lack of knowledge of research techniques. In some of my research in the United States, Canada and the United Kingdom,[3] I have found that practitioners, because of their qualifications and experience, do not generally have a good knowledge of research techniques underlying approaches to evaluation in public relations practice – nor do they believe that knowledge of research techniques is particularly important in their own work and careers. Some believe that public relations is a non-quantifiable service, and that the final test of effectiveness is to be found in client or management satisfaction which work carried out. David Dozier's work in the United States has shown that a large number of practitioners come into public relations with experience in journalism and tend to use techniques of evaluation which are an extension of information gathering methods already familiar to them, such as monitoring news media coverage.[4]

Practitioners nevertheless do need a familiarity with research techniques of use in evaluating public relations activities, their costs, advantages and limitations. Managers and others seeking advice on public relations matters should be able to draw on this knowledge when programmes are being planned, undertaken and reviewed.

The role of research in evaluation – techniques of use in public relations

Public relations is a research-based practice, but the obstacles just discussed may limit the use made of research. What needs to be established through research – formal or informal, depending on resources available – is the impact of public relations activities. The impact sought is an effect upon behaviour, but measures of change in awareness, opinions or attitudes may also be taken. Dr. Lloyd Kirban, in a Burson–Marsteller monograph, [5] makes the point that much of what passes for evaluation in public relations actually measures output from public relations activities rather than their impact. Output may include numbers of publications produced, or amounts of media coverage generated. These measures have some value, but they do not provide an indication of impact. Other steps have to be taken to measure impact. For example, media coverage would need to be followed with measures of response to the coverage.

Three types of research may be necessary at all stages of public relations programmes to measure impact:

- *Formative research*, which establishes bench-marks – preliminary measures – and serves to clarify situations and objectives. Any public relations programme which sets out to increase awareness, change attitudes or behaviour, or bring about any kind of change should be based on research which establishes present levels of awareness, present attitudes or behaviour. This measurement can be used later, at the end of programme activities, to help to assess what changes have taken place. Research prior to programme implementation therefore allows for the measurement of effects. It sets one measure. After programme activities have been undertaken, similar research can be carried out which indicates changes which have taken place. This simple 'pre-test, post-test' design can be misleading in public relations practice because changes may be due to causes other than public relations activities.

  Formative research helps in setting precise and measurable objectives. These are a prerequisite for later evaluation. However, more than research and analysis is involved in setting objectives for public relations programmes, a point to which I shall return

- *Diagnostic research,* which makes it possible to check on, refine or revise objectives and monitor progress towards their achievement. It can include tracking studies, studies of media content to see if important messages are coming through in media coverage, surveys of awareness, opinions or attitudes, to check on whether or not key publics are receiving and responding to messages, or observations of behaviour, to see if information received is contributing to change in attitudes or behaviour.

Diagnostic research answers the questions: Is the programme working in the way intended and, if not, which elements need to be changed to make it work? Do programme objectives need to be modified, and in what way?

■ *Evaluative research*, which looks back to measures established at the outset of activities, and measures changes which have occurred. For example, a programme may have been initiated with the intention of changing awareness of an issue where it may have been established, through survey work before the programme began that awareness of the issue was to be found among only ten per cent of a particular target group. An objective of the programme might be to increase the number of people aware of the issue to 50 per cent, over a predetermined period. Survey work at the end of the programme might discover that awareness of the issue was now to be found among over 50 per cent of the population, and the programme might be judged to have been successful, on this measurement, even though the change measured might be due to factors other than the public relations programme

In practice, evaluation techniques are used to gather as much information as possible, to enable practitioners and managers to decide whether or not programmes have been successful. Research is the basis of evaluation in public relations practice, contributing to programme development (as formative research), to programme refinement (as diagnostic research) and to assessments of programme effectiveness (as evaluation research).

Useful research methods in public relations management

In public relations management, a number of research methods are useful. Research may be informal – 'quick and dirty', an informal sampling of opinion, or a review and summary of previously-published research reports which may have a bearing on the problem now being dealt with – or formal, using some of the more rigorous methods developed for social research, such as surveys and managed work with groups of people acting as focus groups. Research may also be primary or secondary. Secondary research, or desk research, draws on information already available, through other studies or reports, while primary research is research commissioned to examine the problem now being dealt with; it is original research.

Decisions may need to be made about the sort of research that can be done. There are a number of trade-offs to be considered by the manager contemplating the use of research to inform public relations planning and activity. If resources and time are short, informal and secondary research will be more practical, but decisions made on the basis of this research may not be as well-informed as those based on the results of original research carried out to investigate a specific problem.

How much confidence does the manager need to feel in the decisions that are made regarding expenditures on public relations activities and the activities themselves? If there is a need for a high level of confidence, and resources are available, the manager should opt for primary and formal research as a guide to planning public relations activities. An example of this approach is found in the election activities of major political parties. Because the stakes for a political party going into an election are high, some of the resources of the party organization are allocated to regular opinion polling to guide election activities. Party leaders and managers have to have a high level of confidence in decisions that they make regarding election activities, and pay for and use research accordingly.

Other organizations, unwilling or unable to allocate resources to research, have to decide how much accuracy is required in the information that is needed to make decisions. The organization may accept a compromise, using inexpensive secondary research methods and some staff time to gather information, but will make decisions with less confidence. Management decision-making is almost always based on less-than-complete information, in any case.

Quantitative research allows information to be gathered and interpreted using statistical techniques. These techniques allow decision-makers to make decisions from numerical information with known levels of confidence, but there are a number of reasons to be cautious regarding the precision that statistical techniques seem to bring to decision-making. Information expressed numerically, for example, responses on a questionnaire with a series of scales, has lost some of the richness of the original information. Available techniques, such as scales on questionnaires or closed questions allowing for few responses, may exclude important responses. The precision of statistical techniques, which allow for the manipulation of large amounts of information, may be achieved only at the expense of important information which cannot be gathered quantitatively.

Examples of quantitative methods of value in public relations practice include survey methods, making use of questionnaires administered by mail or in face-to-face interviews, and content analysis, which summarizes and draws conclusions from amounts of news media coverage, or from the contents of publications, such as internal newsletters. Content analysis might be used to determine how much coverage had been given to management and employee concerns in an internal newsletter to see if balanced coverage was being provided.

Qualitative methods overcome some of the disadvantages of quantitative methods, but have their own limitations. A qualitative method gathers information that is difficult to interpret. Any two observers may disagree on its meaning, but it does capture a fuller picture of what is happening in social situations under investigation.

Qualitative methods include work with focus groups, in which groups of people are gathered to discuss issues of interest in the research being carried out. The discussion is guided and focussed on the issues by a discussion leader or facilitator, and observers watch the discussion, which is also recorded for later analysis. Focus group work is a useful way of finding out what people think of the issues under discussion, but they may also help researchers understand how members of the groups relate to each other. A focus group might be used to show how employees at different levels in the same organization interact, or to show how participants might work together in a crisis. Other qualitative methods include participant observation, where researchers put themselves into the situation they wish to understand. For example, a researcher may play the part of a customer to see how an organization treats customers.

In public relations practice, decision-making and evaluation are assisted by the use of quantitative and qualitative methods together. If used together, the strengths and weaknesses of each set of methods balance out, so that qualitative information 'colours' the picture which is provided by quantitative approaches which produce statistical summaries. Practically, it is difficult enough to find time and resources to use one approach to evaluation and to have the opportunity to use a number of approaches is rare.

Steps in the evaluation of public relations activities

Step 1
Initiation. Public relations activities – of research, analysis, planning and programme development, implementation and evaluation – are set in motion, as outlined in Chapter 1, by the presentation of an opportunity, problem or difficulty, or in support of an organization's overall objectives.

Step 2

The second step involves a period of negotiation between manager and public relations practitioner, or within the management group, to clarify overall objectives, the situation faced and possible courses of action. This period of negotiation should be informed by research, if this is practical. The period of negotiation is vital in the development of effective public relations programmes. At this stage, agreement should be reached regarding the situation, objectives, appropriate evaluation points and final evaluation.

Step 3

Based on agreement, programme activities can be chosen to achieve agreed objectives. Formative research may be necessary to help to set objectives which are precise and measurable and to test and choose among alternative courses of action.

Step 4

During programme implementation, tracking or other studies can be carried out as activities are carried out. Analysis of media content may be used at this stage to check that messages appearing are those identified as important during earlier discussions of programme content.

Step 5

Programme evaluation. This considers programme objectives, the results of interim measurements of progress towards reaching them and the results of measures of impact on the attitudes and behaviour of key publics.

Evaluation and the techniques used will be specific to the programme and should be decided upon in the preliminary discussions between client or manager and practitioner. Similar programmes will require similar approaches to evaluation. For example, for consumer public relations programmes initiated to support marketing objectives, evaluations which use quantitative measures and examine consumer attitudes and sales figures may be required. Qualitative and intuitive evaluations may be more suitable to check on the effectiveness of public affairs, issues management or government relations programmes.

Measures of public relations' effects

Public relations activities are intended, in the end, to have an impact on behaviour, but other effects may be observed. Measures may be made of changes in behaviour, or of levels of response, or of changes in attitudes, opinions or awareness. Measures of media contents are also commonly used. Measures can be taken of amounts of content generated, which can be costed for comparison with amounts of advertising. Media content can be interpreted, and attempts made to weight the value of media content according to the publications or media in which it appears. For example, judgements can be made about whether or not it is more valuable to appear in a newspaper like Britain's *Financial Times*, or in the financial pages of more popular but less influential daily newspapers.

Other measures of public relations' effects may be more subjective. For example, a programme may be judged effective if clients or sponsoring organization feel satisfied with results achieved, without using any objective measures of the programme. Judgement, intuition and 'gut feeling' can also provide measures of effects.

Studies of the way managers actually work have demonstrated the importance of 'gut feelings', intuition and judgement. Managers constantly make decisions on the basis of hunches, and in the absence of complete information. Public relations managers are no different from other managers in this respect.

Case studies in evaluation

Public relations consultancies and in-house departments with adequate resources will carry out evaluation work as part of public relations activities. A number of consultancies in the United Kingdom interviewed as part of a study by Cranfield School of Management of evaluation practices found that some major consultancies consistently propose formal evaluation work to clients, and conduct research on their own initiative, in order to develop new business. Some consultancies use media monitoring techniques, as a means of checking the performance of account groups, to see whether or not the content of targeted publications included material produced by members of the consultancy staff.

The Burson–Marsteller monograph, *What's the Impact*,[6] contains a number of good examples of the use of research for evaluation purposes. One case included shows how research can be used to evaluate a programme's effectiveness and to improve programme elements. Research followed interviews given by a spokesman on local radio, whose task was to put across a number of important messages about the value of a new type of insurance policy. The research, which involved interviews with a representative sample of local people after the radio item had been broadcast, found that some of the messages were not being received and that some of the details of the new service were not understood. The research results enabled the consultancy to adjust the content of the interviews as they continued, to make sure that important messages were expressed forcefully and in terms that were easier to understand.

In 1985, I was involved in an extensive evaluation of communications programmes managed by the federal department of health and welfare in Canada, in the country's eastern, Atlantic region.[7] The department had set itself the goal of improving awareness of its objectives and programmes in the region, using external and internal communication to do so. Internal communication was to improve staff awareness of departmental programmes, so that they would be able to inform the public about the department.

Evaluation of the department's communication programmes, which were managed in the region by a regional public affairs office, used several surveys:

- A survey, by telephone, of members of the general public in the region, at the beginning and the end of the evaluation period, which was set at six months
- A survey, using face-to-face interviews, of members of the public in the region's largest metropolitan area. This survey, conducted at the end of the evaluation period, supplemented information gathered in the telephone survey and asked more probing questions about the department's programmes
- A survey, using a mailed questionnaire, of department staff in the region. This survey was carried out at the beginning of the evaluation period and at its end

The surveys were intended to find out how aware members of the groups studied were of departmental information and programmes. They were also intended to find out what changes of awareness had taken place over the evaluation period and whether or not these changes could be linked to departmental communication activities. Communication activities of the department in the region during the evaluation period were carefully summarized.

The survey results showed that more members of the general public were aware of the department and its activities at the end of the evaluation period. Within the department, more staff in the region were aware of information from the regional public affairs office, according to measures provided by the second survey of staff at the end of the evaluation period.

The results of the evaluation suggested that public affairs and communications activities were being effective, and they were increasing awareness of the department. A benefit of the survey results was that the department was able to gather a wealth of information about public awareness of the department, which was used as a basis for future programme development.

Some of the findings which were useful for the department's regional management group included:

- A number of current communications activities undertaken by the department were not effective, for example, small information sheets inserted with pension and benefit cheques mailed from the department were not read. Members of the public made little reference to them as sources of information about the department

- The studies showed that advertising and insertion of information in easy-to-read telephone directory entries were effective ways of stimulating awareness of departmental services

- Access to, and design of, departmental offices needed to be improved, so that members of the general public would feel that the offices were more useful as sources of information

- Special training programmes were needed for staff in contact with the general public. The studies found that these staff were no more knowledgeable about the range of departmental services than other members of staff, and yet members of the general public regarded them as important sources of information

- Staff in the department relied heavily on written communication for information about developments within the department. This needed to be improved, and information from the regional public affairs office needed to be brief and current, with details of staff and programme changes, to be most useful

Evaluation of public relations activities can provide a rich source of information for making improvements to services provided. It also has the potential to disturb some comfortably held assumptions about existing programmes and programme elements.

Organizing for evaluation

Evaluation of public relations activities does require a commitment of resources, and allocation of responsibility for evaluation. In a one-person public relations office, or in the work of a public relations consultant, evaluation is one step that needs to be allowed for in carrying out public relations work. In the larger consultancy or in-house department, staff may be given specific responsibilities for evaluation. A consultancy may maintain a research department, or nominate a knowledgeable staff member to be responsible for commissioning research with outside agencies. In-house, within the larger internal public relations department, research staff or a research unit may be established. Staff in the internal department may also draw on other organizational resources, such as a library.

Having staff appointed to research positions means that they are available, as a resource in all programme development work, and for consultation before decisions are made. Their advice can add weight to recommendations made to clients or management. They are also able to provide continuity, for example to carry out work to track the effectiveness of activities over time. Against these advantages, research may be a costly activity, and the appointment of research staff adds significantly to costs.

Summary points

Evaluation is an important issue in public relations. Because public relations is an imprecise practice, questions are raised by clients for public relations services, managers and public relations practitioners themselves regarding the value of public relations activities. The key to evaluation of public relations is to be found in the use of research. Information gathered using more or less formal research methods can be used to judge the effectiveness of public relations. There are obstacles to the use of research in public relations practice, cost being a major one, but it can guide programme development, track the effectiveness of programmes, and help to assess their value on completion. When research cannot be carried out, judgement alone may be used, as it is in other areas of management. There are a number of research techniques of value in assessing the effectiveness of public relations activities, and practitioners need to be familiar with these to underpin the advice given to clients and employing organizations.

Managers need to give thought to organizing for evaluation. Does the organization have sufficient need for research support to justify the appointment of specialist research staff within the public relations department, or should research help be bought in as necessary? If there is need, does the organization have the resources to appoint research staff, and will the benefits of research work outweigh the costs involved?

CHAPTER ELEVEN

SETTING UP THE PUBLIC RELATIONS FUNCTION

READERS OF THE appointments pages in Britain's national newspapers may have noticed a steady increase in the numbers of public relations positions advertised over recent years. Leading newspapers now run special sections to cope with the demand for staff to work in media and creative positions, such as public relations positions. Organizations which have not in the past employed their own public relations staff are now moving to recruit staff to initiate and manage their public relations activities. Practitioners long in place in commercial and consultancy organizations are being joined, in greater numbers, by practitioners working for charitable organizations, educational institutions and health care organizations.

Among the recruitment advertisements, it is not uncommon to see requests for public relations personnel qualified to set up new departments, on a 'green field' site, as one advertisement put it several weeks ago. This chapter will take a look at some of the practical details involved in setting up public relations on a 'green field' site. Should an internal appointment be made, and if so, what qualifications should be sought in applicants? Or should external services be bought in – what is involved in choosing and using public relations consultants? How should the organization budget for public relations activities? What are some of the special problems involved in managing public relations activities? Finally, it will consider some of the characteristics and results of well-managed public relations activities. This chapter will draw together the specialist areas of practice discussed throughout the book to show

how public relations activities can be organized and managed.

Making an internal appointment – or buying in outside help

In Chapter 1, the options for managing public relations were outlined. The decision to make an appointment to a staff position in public relations should follow consideration of:

- The organization's needs: for example, for support from important groups
- The demands being made on the organization from the environment in which it is operating
- The resources on which it can call
- The amount of work likely to be involved in managing important relationships
- The consequences of inattention to the management of those relationships

If, after these points are considered, senior management believes that an internal appointment is necessary, the task of finding a suitably qualified candidate begins. A first step towards appointing to a public relations position is the obvious one of defining the role that the public relations practitioner is to play, preferably by thinking through and developing a job description for the individual. Although this is an obvious step it is one that may be neglected. Robert Mason, writing in the *Harvard Business Review*,[1] suggests that one of the reasons why many organizations become disillusioned by their experience with public relations appointments is that they fail to define the roles of their public relations staff.

One of the difficulties involved in developing job descriptions for public relations positions is that those who have the task of writing them may not understand the scope of public relations. To avoid this difficulty, a public relations consultancy may be asked to help in developing a job description, as a preliminary to recruitment.

Problems which can arise if job descriptions are not thought out properly before recruitment include:

- The job description developed may not allow for important tasks in public relations. For example, a job description which casts the role as that of technician, using communication techniques on behalf of the organization, may exclude the possibility that the practitioner can carry out and interpret research and provide strategic advice to management
- Role problems, where, after an appointment has been made, conflicting or contradictory expectations for the work of the public relations practitioner may create practical difficulties. For example, if line managers see the practitioner as providing technical support for their activities, while senior management view his or her role as that of a personal assistant or adviser to the chief executive officer, the potential conflict of expectations may lead to difficulties for the individual occupying the role. Role problems are not unique to public relations practice, but they can be minimised if careful thought is given to defining and communicating what public roles are to involve

A job description for a public relations position will usually include elements such as:

- A description of the scope of the position
- Details of reporting relationships. Ideally, for a senior public relations position, reporting will be direct to the organization's most senior manager
- A list of duties
- Details of special skills or areas of expertise required. Public relations positions require the exercise of judgement as well as good communication skills.
- Details of qualifications needed. There is a debate among public relations practitioners about the formal qualifications needed for public relations positions. One opinion is

that public relations is by now a practice which requires
entrants to have a degree level qualification. An opposing
view is that the practice demands judgement and shrewd-
ness, which can be developed through relevant experience
and do not necessarily come with a degree or other
qualification

It is likely that public relations will become a graduate
practice in the near future in the United Kingdom. In the
United States, employers can choose from among graduates in
public relations and other disciplines. In the United Kingdom,
public relations is becoming a popular choice of career among
university graduates. Major consultancies, such as Burson-
Marsteller and Shandwick, receive as many as 1,000 applications for the small number of graduate entry positions they
offer each year. According to Tom Parker, director of human
resources in Burson-Marsteller's London office, the consultancy is able to choose a number of able graduates from
leading universities each year.

Degrees in public relations have been widely available for
many years in the United States, but they have only just
become established in the United Kingdom. It will be 1993
before employers in the United Kingdom will have graduates
with these qualifications to consider. In the meantime,
employers such as Burson-Marsteller look for good general
degrees, as well as for degree subjects that match projected
business requirements.

I shall return to qualifications for public relations practice,
but there is one other general question facing employers
seeking to make an appointment to a public relations position.
Should the person appointed to a public relations position be
an individual qualified in the work of the organization making
the appointment, or a qualified public relations practitioner
who can become familiar with its work?

Some companies, such as oil companies or banks, have
established policies for assigning or recruiting staff qualified
by experience in the organization to staff positions such as

public relations positions. Arguments for this approach are that the individual will know the complexities and the sensitivities of the organization's work, and will be able to learn public relations skills more easily than the details of the organization's work.

Against this, public relations practitioners will argue that public relations is itself a specialist practice, and that an individual not having the specialist skills required will not be able to acquire them as easily as some employers might think.

Management will have to decide which approach to recruitment is to be taken. The decision will be influenced by the requirements of the organization and by the amount of time available to it. The organization may need the immediate application of public relations skills, because of some crisis or pressing set of problems. If more time is available, the organization may be able to opt for appointing an individual qualified in some other area who can be trained to develop public relations skills.

What management will be looking for in the individual who is appointed to a public relations position is effectiveness in the role. This is based on:

- Energy
- An ability to tolerate the frustrations of working in an advisory role
- An ability to get things done, and to see projects through to their conclusion, often against tight deadlines
- Good personal presentation skills
- Good interpersonal skills, an agreeable personality and an ability to get on easily with a wide variety of people, at all levels in organizations and outside
- Abilities to communicate well verbally and in writing, and to be persuasive
- Analytical ability, for example to analyse and understand group dynamics, organizational politics and social situations
- Management skills

- Consulting skills
- Judgement

By now, the pattern of education and training for public relations is becoming clear. Public relations practitioners need to have a broad appreciation of the cultures in which they are to work, an ability to analyse social situations, and well-developed communication and management skills. A scheme for the education and training of public relations practitioners developed for the British Public Relations Education Trust suggests that qualified public relations practitioners need to have a broad degree-level preparation for entry into the practice, complemented by early practical experience of using the skills required in practice, such as organizing and communication skills.[2]

Entry should be followed by a thorough training in the requirements of the practice, and further education to develop knowledge of organizations, society and business practice. Further education may involve continuing professional education, an advanced degree in public relations, or – for practitioners intending to practice at the most senior management levels – a further business or management qualification, such as a master's degree in business administration.

Some of the new public relations degrees now available in the United Kingdom do provide potential entrants into public relations practice with a broad education and opportunities to gain practical experience.

Another route into public relations practice is from a first career in other fields, such as journalism, advertising or law. Individuals coming into public relations from other careers will need to be adequately prepared for their new roles, but once they have acquired the skills and knowledge which underlie public relations practice they will have much to offer. The individual qualified in law and public relations, for example, has an advantage in discussing the legal aspects of a crisis or takeover defence, over the practitioner who lacks legal knowledge.

Managers seeking to appoint to a public relations position will need to be confident that the candidates they consider are qualified for it by education, training and experience. At this stage in the development of public relations practice, employers may look for:

- A good general degree, or a degree in public relations which is broad and demanding in content
- Evidence of specific training in public relations (derived from experience with a public relations consultancy with an established training programme, or with in-house public relations departments in companies or other organizations with an enlightened approach to staff development and training)
- Experience appropriate to the level of the position being filled
- Strong evidence of achievement. Did the practitioner's work make a difference?

Studies of career patterns in public relations indicate that training in the requirements of the practice following entry should last for a period of two years. A further three years is needed to bring individuals up to a full working level, where they can confidently manage public relations programmes. Preparation for advanced and specialist work, or for more general and senior management roles, will take a further two or more years.

Typical career progression – some examples

Practitioners now working in public relations follow a number of career paths in public relations. Here are a number of real life but anonymous examples:

- Practitioner A took a law degree and qualified to practise before going into banking. After international and head office experience, he joined an investor relations consultancy and gained public relations skills. As a basis for his future career, he took an advanced management qualification and then moved from public relations consultancy into a senior public relations role with a financial services company

- Practitioner B joined a public relations consultancy as a secretary after taking an arts degree. After a year as a secretary, she became an account executive, and has since progressed, in three years, to the level of account director with another consultancy, where she has responsibility for service to a group of accounts. She is beginning to feel her lack of preparation for management, and her consultancy is providing her with opportunities to attend short courses to build her management skills

- Practitioner C has nearly 20 years of experience in company management, as a personal assistant to the heads of small and large companies. She has an arts degree and a post-graduate qualification in business and secretarial studies. She has recently taken advantage of an opening to take a public relations role in the large company for which she now works, and is developing the public relations skills she lacks, to complement her business and management knowledge

- Practitioner D has recently joined a major public relations consultancy, having just completed a doctorate in a subject relevant to the company's business interests. He is now working through the company's internal training programme, to develop his public relations skills

- Practitioner E began his working life as a journalist and moved into public relations practice with a large, multinational corporation as a junior public relations staff member. Using the experience gained there, he established a one-person consultancy, which grew to become a sizeable business. He has now sold his consultancy and begun another one-person and highly specialised company

In future, the likely career pattern for a public relations

practitioner will include: a first degree in public relations, business, social sciences, arts or communication studies; five years' training running through a similar number of years' experience in the practice, and a further qualification in public relations or management. Practical experience should include experience with a number of organizations, through several levels from entry, through working levels to advanced and managerial levels.

Finding suitable candidates

Advertising public relations positions will usually produce a large number of applicants. Public relations is a practice to which many people are attracted, often for the wrong reasons. It is perceived at a glamorous and exciting occupation, which almost anyone is qualified to take up, especially if they like people. The reality of public relations practice is that it requires good management skills, ability to play close attention to detail, and an unsentimental view of the way people behave. Unsuitable candidates who respond to advertising can be screened out of consideration, but this is time-consuming.

Public relations positions are often filled through the professional grapevine, without the need for advertising. Practitioner groups are still small, even in the countries in which public relations practice is well established, and it is possible to link in to the network of practioners to find out who is available, or to make vacant positions known to potential candidates. Executive search consultancies specialising in public relations can also be drawn upon in the search for potential employees.

Possible candidates, their qualifications and experience, will be judged against the requirements of positions. Employers may want to make use of psychometric tests to gather information to help in decision-making, and they should look at samples of candidates' work, such as programme documents, proposals, printed material, or speeches.

Choosing and using public relations consultancies[3]

Internal staff may be assisted by outside help, provided by public relations consultancies, or, in some organizations, external services may take the place of internal staff. The decision to use outside help instead of making an internal appointment will be influenced by the needs of the organization, management attitudes towards staffing functions such as public relations, the availability of external services, and the organization's resources. External help to assist in the work of an internal department can be called in when:

- There is a special need that can be met with the expertise offered by an outside group, for example at time of defence against a takeover bid
- The volume of work carried by internal staff calls for the temporary employment of additional help
- Internal staff are looking for a new perspective on problems faced, or established programmes
- Services are needed at locations away from the organization's usual places of operation, for example in public affairs work with the European Commission in Brussels

Organizations such as the Public Relations Consultants' Association in the United Kingdom can provide advice on approaching and finding public relations consultants. Consultancies vary in size and in the range and scope of their services. The largest are the multinationals, consultancies such as Burson–Marsteller, Hill and Knowlton, and Shandwick, which are present in most major markets around the world. Another group of consultancies is predominantly national in scope, but capable of acting internationally through membership in networks of consultancies, or through a small number of subsidiary offices, in centres such as Brussels.

Smaller consultancies provide regional or local services, or specialist services, for example in media relations, public affairs or marketing support.

Choosing a consultancy involves careful consideration of the needs of the organization and the scope of the services required. Clients buy time, expertise, support and managerial competence from public relations consultancies, which are specialized service businesses. The service they offer is a problem-solving service delivered through a client-consultancy relationship.

From the client's point of view, a number of questions are important:

- What is the problem or opportunity now presenting itself, which may be dealt with or realized with the assistance of a public relations consultancy?
- What resources does the organization have to commit to work with a public relations consultancy?
- Which consultancies have the staff, expertise and reach to work on the problem or opportunity identified?
- How can a suitable consultancy be chosen?

The problem, opportunity or situation facing the organization can be defined as the basis for a brief, or set of instructions, to a number of public relations consultancies. There is a principle in consulting practice that the presenting problem, or the situation first defined by the client, may not prove to be the problem or siutation that finally has to be worked upon. Clients for public relations services should expect to be questioned closely about their views of the problems they face.

Public relations problems, or situations in which public relations support may valuable, are not easily defined. An organization experiencing difficulties as a result of lack of public awareness of its goods and services may find these problems less easy to define and act upon than problems in production or delivery. The first ability to be assessed in any choice among public relations consultancies is the ability to define and act upon problems. This ability must be based upon a knowledge of business and other organizations and the problems confronting them.

Choosing a public relations consultancy involves:

- Finding a number of consultancies able to work on the problem, situation or organizational needs that have been identified. A short list of consultancies can be drawn up after consultation with organizations such as the Public Relations Consultants' Association or use of directories such as the Hollis directory mentioned in Chapter 4
- Inviting the consultancies chosen to submit a proposal giving their recommendations for an approach to the problem or situation set out in the brief
- Reviewing the proposals received from the consultancies approached. These proposals may be 'pitched', presented in a face-to-face presentation by the consultancies to the client
- Assessing the consultancies themselves: the personalities, qualifications and expertise of staff of the consultancies, and the consultancies as business organizations. Do they have sufficient resources? Are they well staffed, and well-managed?
- Checks with other clients of the consultancies involved, as far as this is practical. Consultancies will usually present the credentials of their staff and details of other projects they have worked on as part of their presentation. Good consultancies will have no hesitation in providing the names of clients who could be contacted for an assessment of their work

The presentation made by the consultancies provides a starting point for the work that is to be done by the consultancy. In consultancy practice, the contract that is agreed between client and consultant is vital, to clarify expectations and commitments that are being made. As has been said earlier, public relations is an imprecise practice, but the contract agreed between client and practitioner provides an opportunity to set out a precise programme of work. What results are expected, at what stage in the programme, and how will progress towards them be monitored? Agreement on these points at the outset of a programme of work will avoid misunderstandings and frustration later.

Common sources of frustration are the time it takes for consultants to become familiar with their client organizations and early lack of results from the relationship.

Clients should expect the following benefits from a collaboration with a public relations consultancy:

- Results, measured against the objectives set for the programme of activities agreed at the outset of the relationship
- Reliable service, that goes beyond work on the immediate demands of the agreed programme and extends into advice regarding problems and opportunities that may arise in the future
- Economic service, which is of genuine value to the organization and provided at an agreed cost

Disputes which may arise regarding the costs of public relations services can be minimized if programmes of activities are agreed at the outset of the relationship and are accurately costed. Public relations consultancies base their fees on allocations of executive time to project and programme work, and costs should reflect the composition of project teams and the amount of time spent on project work by staff at different levels. For example, a project which involves time from some of the consultancy's most senior staff as well as a number of junior staff will be more costly than one which is serviced almost entirely by junior staff. Well-managed consultancies will keep detailed records of time spent on projects and disputes regarding costs should be dealt with drawing on these records.

Public relations management – the mechanics

Managing public relations involves programme and project

management, and the disciplines useful in other areas of management are also valuable in public relations to keep projects on track, to monitor progress and to evaluate results. Special events, for example, such as the opening of a new factory or building, can be managed as projects. Programmes may be aimed at achieving longer-term objectives, such as changing relationships with pressure groups over time. Thinking in programme and project terms is useful in identifying all activities needed to bring programmes and projects to their conclusions. Activities can be charted, and progress towards completing them monitored. Programmes can be established in each of the areas of practice that have been discussed in this book.

Budgeting for public relations activities

A question often asked about public relations management is: Is there some ideal amount which should be spent on public relations activities, as a percentage of an organization's overall expenditure? The short answer is no: expenditures on public relations activities will be determined by the organization's objectives and needs for public relations support, and by the programmes of activity which follow from those objectives and requirements.

Budgets for public relations activities will be developed as objectives and needs for public relations support are identified, and balanced with the resources of the organization. Budgets once developed become a useful instrument for defining and controlling public relations activities. The budget for public relations activities is:

- A statement which summarises the allocation of financial resources to public relations activities
- A financial statement of objectives, tasks and priorities for public relations activities
- A means of communication
- A means of controlling and monitoring public relations activities

As a financial statement of objectives, tasks and priorities the budget can indicate where resources have been allocated. For example, if no resources have been committed to research activities, then it is likely that evaluation, using research techniques, is not a priority. A budget can be a clear indication of priorities.

As a means of communication, budgets can be used to explain the public relations function and its priorities. In discussions with organization members regarding expenditures for public relations activities, budget planning and budgets themselves can be used to develop understanding of public relations.

As a means of controlling and monitoring public relations activities, budgets are invaluable. Expenditures against a public relations budget can be monitored, as a check on progress made towards objectives.

Budgets for public relations activities are best developed for programmes. All costs relating to the achievement of specific objectives can be identified. For example, a community relations programmes aimed at increasing community support for company activities might include elements such as the sponsorship of specific events or organizations, a series of public information meetings, feature articles prepared for the local press and a number of open day events at company facilities. A budget which identified each of these items, and staff time involved, would give a more accurate picture of the cost of the whole programme, than a budget which gathered all sponsorship activities, or all media relations activities, into one budget for the whole public relations department. Programme budgeting also assists in the task of evaluation.

Centralized versus decentralized budgets

Public relations budgets may be centralized or decentralized. There are advantages and disadvantages to either arrangement, which need to be considered as decisions are made regarding the allocation of resources to public relations activities.

Centralized budgets are held within the centre of the organization, planned for and managed centrally. Advantages of the centralized approach are:

■ Budgets are easier to control
■ Control over a central budget gives power over public relations activities in the organization
■ Control over a central budget gives the responsible public relations manager an opportunity to discuss budget requirements and public relations activities with other managers and ties the public relations manager into the budget planning cycle within the organization

A centralized budget for public relations activities has the disadvantages that:

■ It may not be understood by line managers, who may see expenditures on public relations activities as unnecessary central costs, or may not appreciate the benefits or details of expenditures on public relations activities because they are made from 'someone else's budget'
■ It may give rise to resentment on the part of line managers, who do not control expenditures on public relations activities needed to support the achievement of their objectives

Decentralized budgets for public relations activities are dispersed throughout an organization, usually as part of line managers' budgets. To give an example, in an organization serving several regions of the country, a regional manager may have a budget for public relations activities in his or her region. Line managers having control over their own budgets for public relations activities may or may not look to public relations personnel for advice on planning their public relations budgets or expenditures.

Decentralized budgets for public relations activities have the advantages that:

- Line managers can be encouraged to look to public relations personnel for advice on public relations planning and budgeting
- 'It's their money' – line managers will take expenditures from their own budgets more seriously
- Public relations staff will have an opportunity to become more directly involved with line managers in planning for public relations activities and expenditures

Disadvantages of decentralized budgets for public relations activities are that:

- Line managers may be inclined to disregard advice from public relations personnel regarding expenditures from their own budgets
- Because they have a few resources of their own, public relations personnel may have little influence on public relations expenditures
- It becomes more difficult to co-ordinate, manage and control public relations activities

Central control over decentralized budgets may be established by management policy. This may insist that decentralized budgets be set up in consultation with public relations staff. Approval of public relations staff may be required before expenditures can be made from decentralized budgets.

Public relations budgets, because of the nature of public relations practice, should include some allowance for unexpected expenditures. Some 'slack' should be incorporated into public relations budgets, but this may be hard to justify. Budget planning is essential, but it is impossible to foresee all contingencies.

In public relations management, as in other areas of management, it is important to understand the budget planning process in any organization. How budgets are arrived at will give an idea of how organizations carry out their forward planning and set priorities. Where organizations have well-developed budget planning processes in place these can be used as a basis for matching public relations planning and management.

The well-managed, effective public relations function

Studies recently carried out by a team of researchers led by Professor James Grunig of the University of Maryland[4] have identified some of the features of the well-managed and effective public relations department. These include:

- The activities of the department are focused on the groups most important to the organization and are managed strategically, to support the organization as it pursues its strategic objectives
- The department is separated from marketing, but links between public relations and marketing are clear and the relationship between public relations and marketing departments is managed productively
- All public relations activities are managed from the public relations department
- The department has a direct reporting relationship to senior management
- The most senior public relations person acts as a manager, not as a communication technician
- The most senior public relations person has:
  - knowledge of the scope of public relations and its place in management
  - good knowledge of, and competence in, the managerial role
  - a good academic preparation for work in public relations and professional standards of practice
- The department's scope is understood throughout the organization
- The most senior public relations person has power in the organization, derived from membership of the 'dominant coalition', the small group of people in any organization who have the power to direct its activities

The Grunig studies, which have been supported by the International Association of Business Communicators, suggest that evidence of the effects of well-managed public relations activities will be found in assessments of how well the organization is achieving its objectives, while remaining free from outside interference, for example from government or pressure groups. Internally, job satisfaction among employees may be an indication that organizations are managing the important relationship with employees well.

Special problems in the management of public relations

Public relations is a relatively new addition to the tasks of management. At this stage in its development there are some specific problems which may be encountered in the management of public relations and which need to be considered:

- As a relatively new function, public relations may not be well understood, and efforts must be made by public relations staff, and by managers who understand the scope of the function, to explain what public relations can contribute
- Staffing and location in the organization. Job descriptions, as we have seen, may not be well defined. The function may not be considered important, or staffed with individuals who are qualified to work in public relations and at an appropriate level
- Lack of management skills on the part of public relations practitioners. A number of studies, including my own which were mentioned at the end of Chapter 10, have established that managerial abilities become increasingly important as individuals progress in a career in public relations. At the present stage in the development of public relations practice, it is recognized that practitioners currently active are not, as a group, particularly able managers. A report on careers in public relations in the *Financial Times* of 17 October 1990, makes the point that

managerial ability among public relations practitioners is still quite low, and that talented new entrants to the practice have the opportunity to shine early in their careers. This situation is changing in the United Kingdom, but it is generally recognized as true that public relations practitioners do not have the same level of knowledge and skill in management as managers in other areas

- Difficulties in setting precise and measurable objectives for public relations activities
- Difficulties in measuring results and effectiveness
- Programme complexity. This arises because of the number of variables, groups and relationships which may have to be taken into account as priorities are decided and programmes planned
- External pressures, for example, from media interest in organization activities. These pressures are felt most immediately in the public department, where routine tasks may be obstructed by crises
- Staff – line problems. Not unique to public relations, these problems arise out of differences between staff and line personnel. Line personnel are responsible for the core activities of the organization, and staff personnel work to advise and support them. The authority of the two groups differs, and line personnel may sceptical of the value of staff personnel to the organization
- Ethical questions. These may be prompted by the use of information by the organization, and by management. An article in the *Harvard Business Review*[5] on ethics in public relations practice suggests that each company has its own 'ethical threshold' and decisions are made by executives on the basis of what they think the threshold is, and their own threshold. The article suggests that public relations performs the function of keeping management in line. Public relations is seen as an anvil against which management morals can be hammered. This role for public relations is not one that is widely accepted, but the practice raises ethical issues which need to be addressed. These bear on

the management of the function

- Difficulties involved in developing a capacity for prediction. Adequate information systems must be in place and readily accessible to the public relations department so that it can alert the organization to changes in the environment, among key groups and in important relationships
- 'Trespassing'. This problem arises when staff from other areas or other functions within the organization trespass on the responsibilities of the public relations department
- Management problems arising from the tasks of managing creative people, and managing a number of external services. Again, the management problem of working with creative people is not unique to public relations practice, but the difficulty in practice is that of creating a work environment and teams in which necessary controls can be introduced without inhibiting the creativity of staff

Organizing for public relations

Organization structure is partly a matter of choices made by senior management groups, and questions regarding organization for public relations management will often need to be taken to the most senior management groups for resolution. In practice, it may be found that, within these groups, overall direction for the organization has not been set clearly enough to guide managers responsible for public relations activities. For example, if a multinational company has not determined its strategy for the single European market of 1992, it will be impossible for the company to decide, in any detail, how it should manage its relations with the European Economic Community Commission, or what it might communicate to employees of its French or Italian subsidiaries.

Public relations should fit into the organization structure in a direct reporting relationship with the organization's senior manager. The senior manager responsible for public relations should be a member of the dominant group in the organization, but should be able to work through all of its levels. The public relations department should be organized around programmes managed, or in relation to groups of special, strategic interest.

Where external services take the place of some, or even all internal staff, the individuals providing service should report in to the senior public relations manager, or members of his or her staff, or to the organization's senior management group.

Setting up the public relations function – summary points

Setting up the public relations function depends upon an understanding of public relations' role in management. This understanding enables choices to be made regarding suitable candidates for public relations positions, staffing the public relations function and choosing external services. Suitable candidates for public relations positions will need to be adequately qualified, through academic preparation, training and experience. Their abilities will need to include strong analytical, interpersonal, communication and management skills.

External services are available from public relations consultancies, which are service businesses offering problem-solving capabilities. They need to be chosen on the basis of performance, credentials, reputation, consulting and problem-solving abilities.

Budgets can be used in public relations management as an important management tool, to communicate priorities for public relations activities and to monitor and evaluate progress. Programme budgeting allows costs relating to the achievement of specific objectives to be identified, and is another important aid to evaluation.

Well-managed public relations departments within organizations have a number of features. They relate directly to senior management, and are headed by qualified practitioners having good managerial abilities as well as membership of the organization's dominant coalition. As a relatively new function, public relations management presents a number of special problems, which follow from persisting lack of understanding of the scope of the function and the shortage of qualified managers able to direct it. These problems, some of which are by no means unique to public relations, will diminish over time.

In public relations management, much depends on the attitudes towards the practice held by senior management, who will make the key decisions regarding the location of the function, and its importance, in the organization.

POSTSCRIPT

Public relations is likely to increase in importance as a task of management over the coming years, for a number of reasons. The environment of the organization – business and government, large and small – is becoming more complex, and groups outside the organization are becoming more demanding. Business organizations are now expected to meet social and political objectives, as well as those of profit and employment. Governments are expected to provide economic stability, steadily-rising standards of living, and solutions to a large number of pressing social problems, such as disparities in opportunity available to different groups of people in society.

The overall task of management is changing. Three great themes in management practice have emerged over the past ten years and will have to be responded to with significant changes in management practice. The first concerns managerial response to international developments, increased international competition and responsibilities. Even the small local business now has to be aware of the activities of competitors in countries remote from the immediate location of the business. Legislation and regulation developed in government centres other than national centres also have to be recognized and obeyed.

The second great theme is environmentalism. For the foreseeable future, concern for the environment and for the impact of business and other activities on it will affect managerial freedom to act. Already, evidence is building that companies are being judged on their performance in safe-guarding the environment. Some have tried to use their early efforts to show concern for the environment to commercial advantage, but much more will be expected in the next few years as more stringent actions to protect the environment become necessary.

The third theme is that of social responsibility. Organizations will be called upon to play a social role beyond immediate objectives, and new collaborations between business, government and voluntary sector organizations will be required. Managers will have to take their social responsibilities, the need to consult with other organizations, public and special interest group concerns into account as they make decisions. The managerial role will become much more political, in the sense that the manager will have to appreciate and balance a variety of interests, while still pursuing and attaining organizational objectives.

In this new role, the manager will need the assistance of advisers who can help to make sense of social complexity, and who can act to clarify interests and influence important groups. These advisers will include qualified and skillful public relations practitioners, but the role and scope of public relations in management are still to be appreciated fully. This book will have served its purpose if it helps managers to make better use of their public relations advisers and to realize the benefits of well-managed public relations activities.

REFERENCES AND NOTES

Chapter 1

1. 'Riches paint poor PR image', *The Times*, 18 July 1990.
2. 'Corporate eyes, ears and mouths', *The Economist*, 16–24 March 1989.
3. 'The Image of Public Relations', The President's Lecture, delivered by Robert M Worcester, Market Opinion Research International, The Institute of Public Relations, 15 July 1987.
4. Public Relations Society of America Terminology Report, October 1988.
5. *Ibid.*
6. 'Management Consultancy, A Survey', *The Economist*, 13 February 1988.

Chapter 2

1. James Grunig and Todd Hunt (1984) *Managing Public Relations*, New York: Holt, Rhinehart & Winston.
2. Roy Eales *Air Canada: Organizing for Public Relations and Media Relations*, Case Number 9–586–144, available from the Case Clearing House of Great Britain and Ireland, Cranfield Institute of Technology, Cranfield, Bedford MK43 OAL, England or HBS Case Services, Harvard Business School, Boston MA 02163, United States.

Chapter 3

1. Theon Wilkinson (Ed.) 1989) *The Communications Challenge: Personnel and PR Perspectives*, The Institute of Personnel Management, United Kingdom.
2. Moreen Traverso and Jon White (1990) 'The Launch of the Prudential's Corporate Identity: A Case Study', in Danny Moss (Ed.) *Public Relations in Practice, A Casebook*, London: Routledge.
3. 'Dow Canada: Avoiding Potential Adverse Reactions by Handling a Situation with Sensitivity and Good PR Practice, Case No. 2014', *Public Relations News*, New York
4. Robert R Blake and Jane S Mouton (1978) *The New Managerial Grid*, Houston: Gower Publishing Co.
5. Theon Wilkinson (Ed.) (1989) *op. cit.*, p. 109.
6. Andrzeij Huczynski (1983) *Encyclopedia of Management Development Methods*, Gower Publishing Co.
7. Carol Reuss and Don Silvis (Eds.) (1981) *Inside Organizational Communication*, New York and London: Longman.

Chapter 4

1. Daniel J. Edelman Limited (1987) *Face the Facts: Freeze the Tax*, Public Affairs Category Winner, Sword of Excellence Awards, Institute of Public Relations. Reported in *Public Relations*, Autumn 1987.
2. Joseph F Coates (1986) *Issues Management: How You Can Plan, Organize and Manage for the Future*, Maryland, USA: Lomond Publications Inc.
3. Public Relations Consultants Association, Willow House, Willow Place, London SW1P 1JH (Tel: 071–233–6026).
4. *Hollis Press and Public Relations Annual*, published annually by Hollis Directories Limited, Contact House, Lower Hampton Road, Sunbury-on-Thames, Middlesex TW16 5HG, England (Tel: 0932–784781).

Chapter 5

1. 'Selling Public Confidence in Sellafield', *Public Relations*, October 1989.
2. Milton Friedman (1970) 'The Social Responsibility of Business is to Increase its Profits', *New York Times* Magazine, 13 September.
3. Mary Lowengard (1989) 'Community Relations: New Approaches to Building Consensus', *Public Relations Journal*, October.
4. 'The Square Mile Project', *Public Relations*, October 1989.

Chapter 6

1. 'How Now, IR?', *Public Relations Journal*, April 1989.
2. Neil Ryder and Michael Regester (1989) *Investor Relations*, London: Business Books.
3. Thomas E Burke (1990) 'Why Investor Relations Counsel Works', *International Public Relations Review*, Vol. 13, No. 1.
4. 'How 5 million people said YES: the TSB Group plc Flotation', *Public Relations*, Vol. 6, No. 1, Autumn 1987.
5. 'The Ministry of Defence', *The Financial Times*, 24–27 September 1986.
6. 'Fallen Stars of the City Pages', *Business*, March 1988.
7. 'Water Privatization: The Marketing and Communications Campaign, Dewe Rogerson', *Public Relations*, Vol. 9, No. 2, 1990.

Chapter 7

1. Philip Kotler and William Mindak (1978) 'Marketing and Public Relations', *Journal of Marketing*, October; Philip Kotler (1986) 'Megamarketing', *Harvard Business Review*, Vol. 64, No. 2.
2. Geert Hofstede (1980) 'Angola Coffee – or the Confrontation of an Organization with Changing Values in its Environment', *Organization Studies, 1/1*.

3. Jon White *Dunhill Holdings: A Case Study in Growth, Acquisition and Marketing Communications*, Case Number 588.002.1, available from the Case Clearing House of Great Britain and Ireland (see address in references to Chapter 2).

4. Simon Caulkin (1990) 'Dangerous exposure: Companies like Perrier have learnt that public relations can decide the fate of a business in crisis', *Best of Business International*, Autumn.

5. W J Keegan (1974) 'Multinational Scanning: A Study of Information Sources Utilised by Headquarters Executives in Multinational Companies', *Administrative Science Quarterly*, Vol. 19, No. 3.

Chapter 8

1. Roberta Wohlstetter (1962) *Pearl Harbor: Warning and Decision*, California: Stanford University Press.

2. 'How Sotheby's Escaped the Hammer', *The Sunday Times*, 8 May 1983.

3. Michael Regester (1989) *Crisis Management: What To Do When The Unthinkable Happens*, London: Business Books.

4. Leonard Snyder (1983) 'An Anniversary Review and Critique : The Tylenol Crisis', *Public Relations Review*, Vol. IX, No. 3.

5. Michael Regester (1989) *op. cit.*

Chapter 9

1. T J Peters and T H Waterman Jnr (1982) *In Search of Excellence: Lessons from America's Best Run Companies*, New York: Harper & Row.

2. Geert Hofstede (1978) 'Culture and Organization: A Literature Review Study', *Journal of Enterprise Management*, Vol. 1.

3. Warren G Bennis (1969) *Organization Development: Its Nature, Origins and Prospects*, Reading, Massachusetts: Addison-Wesley.

4. Wally Olins (1990) *The Corporate Personality*, The Design Council.

5. Graham Cleverley (1973) *Managers and Magic*, Harmondsworth: Penguin Books.

Chapter 10

1. Walter K Lindenmann (1988) 'Beyond the Clipbook', *Public Relations Review*, December.
2. Walter K Lindenmann (1990) 'Research Evaluation and Measurement: A National Perspective', *Public Relations Review*, Vol. 16, No. 2, Summer.
3. Jon White and Greg Trask (1982) *Professional Development Needs Analysis: Canadian Public Relations Practitioners*, Canadian Public Relations Society; Jon White (1987) *Professional Development Needs Analysis: Institute of Public Relations Members*, London: Institute of Public Relations; Jon White, Frank Kalupa and Linda Hammonds (1987) 'Professional Development Needs Analysis: A Study of US Communication Practitioners', paper presented to the Association for Education in Journalism and Mass Communication Conference.
4. David Dozier (1989) 'The Innovation of Research in Public Relations Practice', *Public Relations Research Annual*.
5. Dr Lloyd Kirban (1984) 'What's the Impact', *Burson–Marsteller Monograph*, New York.
6. *Ibid*.
7. 'Evaluation Project on Communications, Health and Welfare, Canada, Atlantic Region', April 1985.

Chapter 11

1. Robert S Mason (1974) 'What's a PR Director For, Anyway?' *Harvard Business Review*, September–October.
2. 'Scheme for the Education and Training of UK Public Relations Practitioners', a working paper prepared for the Public Relations Education Trust, Cranfield School of Management, 1987.
3. The Institute of Directors (1988) *Director's Guide to Choosing and Using a PR Consultancy*, London: The Institute of Directors.

4. James Grunig (1990) 'Excellence in Public Relations and Communications Management', remarks to the 1990 International Conference of the International Association of Business Communicators, Vancouver, Canada.
5. D Finn (1959) 'The Struggle for Ethics in Public Relations', *Harvard Business Review*, January–February.

INDEX